KEYS TO THE MARKETPLACE:

PROBLEMS AND ISSUES IN CULTURAL AND HERITAGE TOURISM

EDITED BY
PATRICIA ATKINSON WELLS

D1477596

HISARLIK PRESS
1996

Published by Hisarlik Press, 4 Catisfield Road, Enfield Lock, Middlesex EN3 6BD, UK. Georgina Clark-Mazo and Dr Jeffrey Mazo, publishers.

British Library Cataloging-in-Publication data available.

ISBN 1 874312 31 1

10 9 8 7 6 5 4 3 2 1

Printed in Great Britain by Watkiss Studios Ltd.

Contents

The Authors

Linda Caldwell is Executive Director of the Tennessee Overhill Heritage Tourism Association.

Robert Cogswell is Director of the Folk Arts for the Tennessee Arts Commision.

Simon Goudie is a researcher and consultant based at the Environmental Advisory Unit, University of Cape Town.

Clodagh Brendan Harvey is a freelance Heritage Consultant in Northern Ireland.

Keith Hollinshead is Assistant Professor, Tourism Sciences, Department of Recreation, Park and Tourism Sciences, Texas A&M University.

Benita J. Howell is Associate Professor and Associate Head of the Anthropology Department, University of Tennessee, Knoxville.

Farieda Khan is the Projects Director of the Environmental Advisory Unit, University of Cape Town.

Daryll Kilian is a consultant at the Environmental Advisory Unit, University of Cape Town.

Francesca McLean is Director of Folklife Programs for the Montana Arts Council.

Josey Petford is a post-graduate student at the Roehampton Institute, London.

Jean Haskell Speer is Director of the Center for Appalachian Studies and Services and Professor of Anthropology at East Tennessee State University.

Patricia Atkinson Wells is Publications Editor for the College of Business, Middle Tennessee State University, and Co-Principal in Heritage Partnerships, a cultural tourism consulting group.

Caroll Van West is Assistant Professor and National Register Projects Coordinator at the MTSU Center for Historic Preservation.

PREFACE

As a folklorist, my education, avocations, and varying employment have led me to span the usual intradisciplinary divides, and I stand—sometimes precariously—with one foot firmly in the camp of academic folklore and the other in that of the public sector. I find myself increasingly drawn to and working in applied ethnology, both at the grassroots level—as in my work providing technical assistance in the areas of business skills, promotion and marketing to traditional artists and performers, and at the policy-making level—lobbying state agencies and the tourism industry on behalf of the arts, rural community development and cultural and heritage tourism.

This present volume is both a reflection and a result of this alternate micro-macro view of ethnology and the marketing of traditions. It had its inception in an issue of *Tennessee's Business*, the thrice-yearly publication of the Business & Economic Research Center at Middle Tennessee State University. Although as a folklorist I am an anomaly in the College of Business (where I am employed as Publications Editor), the position affords me access to different perspectives and some unusual partnerships in terms of research and public service projects.

With the issue of *Tennessee's Business*—"Preserving and Promoting Cultural Resources: Strengthening Local Economies Through Responsible Tourism"—my intent was to get the perspectives of folklorists, anthropologists, historians, and community organizers to the people who have the money and power to affect policy—the business community, elected representatives, and government officials. The issue was so well-received that it went out of print in less than a year; budgetary constraints did not permit reprinting.

At this time, I began to seek a publisher and to conceive of adding some substantial essays of international interest and import. I am delighted that Hisarlik Press decided to take on this project, and that I have been able to gather essays on cultural and heritage tourism outside the USA from scholars in the fields of applied anthropology, public folklore, natural resource management, and tourism research to supplement the original group of papers.

I would be remiss if I did not thank Dr Reuben Kyle, Director of the Business & Economic Research Center at MTSU, and Dr Teri F. Brewer of the University of Glamorgan, without whose support and encouragement this volume would not have seen print. My thanks also to the authors—scholars and gentlepeople every one—for putting their work in my hands.

PATRICIA ATKINSON WELLS
MURFREESBORO, TENNESSEE

Acknowledgements

Chapters 1, 6, 7, 9 and 10 are reprinted with permission from *Tennessee's Business*, Volume 8 No. 1, *Preserving and Promoting Cultural Resources: Strengthening Local Economics Through Responsible Tourism.* Murfreesboro, TN: Business & Economic Research Center, Middle Tennessee State University, 1995.

Chapter 2 is an updated version of a previously published article, "First-Blush of the Longtime: The Market Development of Australia's Living Aboriginal Heritage," *Tourism Research: Expanding Boundaries,* Proceedings of the 19th Annual Conference (Montreal, Canada, June 1988). Salt Lake City, UT: Travel and Tourism Research Association, 183–98, and is used with permission.

Parts of Chapter 3 originally appeared in "Fool's Gold: Filthy Luce," *Causeway Cultural Traditions Journal* (Winter 1995) and are used with permission.

The cover photograph of a signpost at Siwa Oasis, Egypt, was provided by Josey Petford.

INTRODUCTION

PATRICIA ATKINSON WELLS

Public folklorists in the United States have long been plagued with the problems inherent in successfully presenting the culture of individual "folk" groups to the larger, dominant American culture. While audiences/consumers desire to be included in "private" culture, the folklorist as presenter/interpreter must respect the beliefs and wishes of the people whose culture is being presented. As the context and function of the particular tradition are changed through the act of presentation, what may have been private becomes public. This negotiation between the public and private in presenting cultures often creates a new product or form that could be called "public culture"—a mediated, interpreted, and "packaged" version of custom or tradition that both the esoteric and exoteric participant can be comfortable with. Thus what we have in exhibits and festivals of folklife is really a "product." Cultural resources, or "traditions," are the raw materials from which selection is made. These selected resources are converted into products through interpretation, through a form of storytelling. What is transmitted, and the means of transmission, become the product.

As I began to familiarize myself with the literature of heritage tourism, I became aware that the same transformation processes apply to the creation of "heritage" from history. In the well-established dialogue on "heritage" and the "heritage industry" in Britain, I found numerous issues and concerns that parallel those of public folklorists. In climates (or pockets) of economic decline, people look to exploitable resources for potential economic benefit. The natural environment, the past, and traditional culture are among those resources currently being exploited by communities, governments, and the tourism industry.

What are the goals for producing the cultural or heritage "tourism product?" Who benefits? Who chooses what is to be preserved and what is to be interpreted for public consumption? What kinds of cultural intervention and appropriation are part of this process? Who "owns" culture or heritage? Who endows value on sites, objects and/or activities? What is "authentic" and who decides? Does "commodification" equal "commercialization," "degradation," or "Disneyfication" of the sites, objects, or customary behaviors? What is "sustainable tourism" and to what degree are protection and preservation part of the package? These are among the problems and issues addressed by the authors of the essays in this volume.

In the opening essay, "Doing Right by the Local Folks," Robert Cogswell examines the potential effects of the marketing of culture and heritage on the communities or groups being promoted. Community resources and relations are essential concerns in the growing field of cultural tourism, and they require alternative approaches to tourism development. As the local "way of life" becomes the object of marketing, planning must include cultural expertise, careful assessment, and broad community involvement. According to Cogswell, quality programs will pursue long-range strategies, interpret and present local culture well, and effectively manage the presence of tourists in the community. Including cultural conservation measures and sensitivity to community life among priorities should be seen as compatible with tourism business interests.

Problems of indigenous people and tourism development are central to several of the essays found in this collection. Keith Hollinshead examines the burgeoning Australian tourism trend of the presentation and interpretation of "Black Australia," bringing interdisciplinary perspectives to bear on the complex political, cultural, environmental and economic issues involved in the development of Aboriginal tourism. Stating that it is "imperative for those responsible for marketing decisions to forge healthy relationships with traditional and emergent Aboriginal groups," Hollinshead offers a set of "propositions" to guide tourism operators and practitioners who seek to promote Aboriginal Australia.

Politics, Economics and "Tradition" in Ireland are the subtitle and subject of Clodagh Brennan Harvey's essay "The Heritage Embroglio." Tourism has played a central role in Ireland's economy and cultural life for over a century. The continuing development of international tourism in the latter part of the 20th century has lead to the emergence of a remarkable number of representations of Ireland's material and non-material culture. Harvey takes the reader on an excursion through important heritage attractions in the Two Irelands—North and South—to address salient cultural, economic and political issues.

Simon Goudie, Farieda Khan and Darryll Kilian examine some of the key debates and controversies related to the inclusion and empowerment of black South Africans in the tourist industry. Black empowerment, they argue, necessarily extends beyond attempts to promote more equitable business partnerships, and should include active strategies to promote awareness of previously neglected or repressed dimensions of black cultural heritage.

The commercial imperative for the tourist industry to continually deliver new and different attractions and destinations for the jaded "been there, done that" tourist often relegates concerns about possible environmental and cultural impacts of tourism to the bottom of the list in development priorities. In her essay "Pushed to the Limits," Josey Petford examines the connection between cultural and economic exploitation through comparative case studies in "neocolonialism" in Siwa Oasis, Egypt and South Wales in Britain.

The southern highlands of the United States, including Appalachian Tennessee, have long been an important tourist destination. Significant issues of cultural identity, cultural hegemony, and the relationship of culture to economic and public policy emerge from critical study of tourism in Appalachia. In her essay "Cultural Tourism in Appalachian Tennessee," Jean Haskell Speer examines major periods of tourism development in the region, the current status of tourism in Appalachia, and possible scenarios for future development of tourism in the region.

Heritage tourism is an economic development strategy that calls upon the skills of both historic preservationists and economic planners. Listing in the (American) National Register of Historic Places makes properties eligible for federal financial incentives and provides local communities with building blocks of resources ideal for development in heritage tourism plans. Carroll Van West's essay "Building Blocks for New Economic Opportunities" reports on three successful pilot projects of the Center for Historic Preservation (at Middle Tennessee State University) that used the National Register listing process as the beginning steps toward more comprehensive economic development plans which utilized heritage tourism and preservation tax incentives.

"Blackfeet Cultural and Economic Development through Tribal Arts," by Francesca McLean, looks at the Blackfeet of Montana, whose traditional lands form part of what is now Glacier National Park. Although approximately two million people pass through the reservation each year on their way to the park, the Blackfeet reap little economic benefit from the tourism dollars spent on or near the reservation. McLean reports on an on-going project of the Blackfeet to simultaneously protect and encourage cultural identity and to develop and manage local natural resources though the production of tribal arts and cultural programming for tourist consumption.

In 1989 the National Trust for Historic Preservation, with support from the national Endowment for the Arts, inaugurated its Heritage Tourism Initiative. Sixteen pilot areas in four states—Indiana, Tennessee, Texas, and Wisconsin—participated in a three-year demonstration program to test the partnership of tourism and preservation. In the Tennessee Overhill area, the development of cultural tourism has resulted in new attractions, new events, historic preservation, economic development, and new partnerships. In her essay "Heritage Tourism—A Tool for Economic Development," project director Linda Caldwell provides a first-personal narrative account of the Overhill experience.

Rounding out the collection, Benita J. Howell examines "Heritage Tourism and Community Development: Lessons from Historic Rugby." Longevity and accomplishments make Historic Rugby, Inc. (Tennessee) an exemplar of well-managed heritage tourism. Historic preservation has always been paramount. Federal protection, a comprehensive Master Plan, and quality interpretation have helped secure grants to fund expansion. Economic development to support a community in this sparsely populated part of the Cumberland Plateau remains a challenge, but controlled growth is in any case desirable to protect qualities that attract visitors and new residents.

These ten essays render a somewhat kaleidoscopic view of the current scholarship on cultural and heritage tourism. The geographic and disciplinary range of the authors and their subjects provides a rich variety of perspectives and approaches. The collection is by no means exhaustive. Worldwide, as regions, states, and communities increasingly look to heritage or cultural tourism for economic opportunities, the challenge to balance the preservation of cultural, historic, and natural resources with the development and marketing of tourism will only become greater.

1

Doing Right By the Local Folks: Grassroots Issues in Cultural Tourism

Robert Cogswell

On the surface, tourism appears to be a simple proposition, especially for communities newly interested in entering alternative tourism markets: outsiders, in response to promotional encouragement, visit an out-of-the-way locale and spend money. This is, no doubt, an attractive scenario for communities hard-pressed for other avenues of economic development, promising to inject new money into the local economy with little capital investment.

But in many ways, tourism development is not so simple as it appears, for it entails a great deal more than conventional business concerns. Its pitfalls and controversies have made news on many levels. In Egypt, Islamic fundamentalists, incited by tourist behaviors that conflict with their own cultural codes, have waged a terrorist campaign against foreign visitors with disastrous results for that country's tourism industry ("When taming..." 1992; Gubernick 1993; Fletcher 1993; "Staying Away..." 1994). In south Florida, highly publicized crimes against international tourists have created a similar crisis (Fedarko 1993; Stoker 1993). In Virginia, the proposal for development of the Disney America theme park on the Mananas battlefield site has recently sparked public debate over appropriate uses of culturally significant properties and interpretations of heritage subject matter (Abney 1994; Wiener 1994). Here in Tennessee, the thriving tourism destination in Sevier County has received criticism for the pay levels and seasonality of its employment opportunities, the pressures it exerts on community infrastructures, and the tourist dollars that do not remain locally (M. Smith 1989; Humphrey 1989; Arnow 1991).

As locales outside of Tennessee's established tourist centers pursue tourism opportunities, governmental, free enterprise, and not-for-profit entities need to be realistic about the potentials for both problems and benefits in tourism development. The alternative approach of "cultural" or "heritage" tourism has spawned a new wave of interest in cultivating smaller-scale and out-of-the-way markets. In the few years since these terms have entered tourism lingo, they have come to encompass a range of tourism motives differing from the more conventional incentives of recreational and scenic (or "eco-") tourism. They have brought new history, arts, and humanities connections into the tourism mix and opened the way for the packaging of old buildings, mom-and-pop events, and "local color" as tourist attractions. The culture and heritage focus brings new themes, new locales, and new people into the tourism industry, all at the same time. If ever there was equal promise for success or disaster—or a need for careful planning—cultural tourism presents it.

While Americans have long been drawn to other countries to experience and enjoy cultural aspects of place, there is a certain irony in this form of tourism having been so recently recognized as an "alternative" within our own country. As local tourism industries develop around it, pursuit of innovative alternatives is one of the keys to successful planning. For more out-of-the-way, culturally distinct, and lesser-populated places where such tourism holds promise, the dominant business models in American tourism—such as those geared toward the major destination, the theme park, or blockbuster celebration—are neither appropriate nor particularly useful.

Where will the alternative ideas come from? Looking in places where cultural tourism has a more extensive track record would be a good place to start. Many of the field's core issues, from overcoming inadequacies in service infrastructures to needs arising from intercultural contact, have in fact already been experimented with and closely studied in Third-World situations. Although the American tourism business remains largely unaware of it, the resultant literature on the "anthropology of tourism" offers a wealth of alternative models, approaches, and insights for cultural tourism development on the American landscape (see for example, de Kadt 1979; V. Smith 1989; V. Smith and Eadington 1992).

Business people can be extremely touchy about the prospects of alternatives, and some of them are prone to dismiss the perspectives of cultural specialists as being "antidevelopment." The gap between the tourism business and various cultural fields is one that will have to be better bridged as the cultural tourism industry matures. In trying to do that, I've found it most useful to point out that culturally productive alternatives do not necessarily conflict with business interests. In fact, most of them make good business sense in the long run.

Some of these alternatives may go against fairly sacred priorities in the tourism business, particularly against the idea that promotion is everything. In one of the first informed overviews of cultural tourism planning, Richard Roddewig identified this widely-held assumption as a major obstacle to improvement. How many tourism officials, he asks, "are consciously developing a strategy to develop this form of tourism, not just market it?" (Roddewig 1988). Roddewig suggests thorough identification and assessment of cultural tourism resources, involvement of people with cultural expertise in planning, and enhancement of weak elements as parts of the development strategy that should be in place long before the advertising.

There's no doubt that marketing is essential to tourism. In fact, when community representatives ask me for advice about starting up cultural tourism, I try to broaden the concept of promotion in what I usually tell them first: selling the host community on the value of cultural tourism, and keeping them sold on it, is as important as selling outsiders on the community as a tourist destination. And by "selling the community," I don't mean superficial PR. I mean a process that combines research and development with public relations, involving the community in the planning and remaining accountable to it, encouraging local self-discovery and pride, and building in incentives for a broad coalition of local interests. Why is this process so important? Because the heritage or way of life defining the tourism draw is, in a real sense, a community property, and because public consensus, especially in smaller-scale and rural contexts, can make or break the entire venture.

The most convincing support for this point of view, which should be required cultural tourism reading, is a non-fiction case study by broadcast journalist Ron Powers entitled *White Town Drowsing*. In chronicling the saga of the Mark Twain Sesquicentennial Celebration in Hannibal, Missouri, Powers masterfully captures the ebb and flow of an extended encounter between slick tourism promotion and small-town America. Most of all, the book successfully portrays the real challenges of cultural tourism planning, from the distractions of get-rich-quick scheming, inflated boosterism, and factional in-fighting, to the ultimate lesson that, despite years of well-motivated planning from the top, lack of community-wide commitment to the enterprise can undermine it (Powers 1986).

The Tourism Product

Even among the people currently talking so much about cultural and heritage tourism, there are differing ideas about what, exactly, these fields are marketing. From the suppliers' side, the mix is currently influenced by various interest groups, most notably in the not-for-profit sector. Historic preservationists, looking in part to increase visitation revenues at sites they maintain, started the current trend in tourism among these constituencies (Fromer 1988; "Looking Forward..." 1988; "Getting started" 1993). Under "heritage," they have stressed promotion of attractions associated with the past of a given destination, such as buildings and other sites, museums, memorials, tours, and sometimes events. The more conservative and established part of this market emphasizes physical associations with local heroes or claims to national fame (from birthplaces or battlefields to "Washington slept here"). Progressive attractions tend to highlight more subtle aspects of the tangible environment (such as the quality of historic architecture on Main Street) or more widely representative and abstract aspects of history (like period "living history" presentations).

Arts activists comprise the other main constituency interested in this area of tourism, and in it they see potential for fund-raising and other assistance in their efforts to sustain and enhance the arts environment of their community (a good overview is Moskin and Guettler 1988). They offer visitors entertainment and enrichment attractions (through local arts facilities, performances, and events), and like their local history counterparts, they are entering the area of retail sales once dominated by entrepreneurial tourism businesses. Except for occasional use of local subject matter (as in outdoor dramas), most of the artistic products they offer are not particularly unique to their locale, but rather are typical of the mainstream American arts market.

From the demand standpoint, on the other hand, one of the fundamental assumptions behind development in this field is that there are tourism consumers "who want to experience a culture, a way of life, on a trip" (Roddewig 1988: 2). The demand reflects the current popularization of "cultural diversity" in America, which is clearly observable in different localities and social groups, but which as an idea has historically taken second place to notions of "America-as-melting-pot." Diversity and sameness, in fact, coexist on different levels of culture in all parts of our country, and tourism planners trying to address the "way of life" market need to ask how well their product represents what is really distinctive about the culture and heritage of their place.

I should be quick to note that, as a tourism product, "way of life" is a very elastic catch-phrase, embracing things much easier to promote than to deliver. From the frequent use of commercialized "sideshow" approaches to cultural exposition in the past—featuring costumed characters repeating staged routines against simulated backdrops—the tourism industry does not have a particularly good track record for appropriate and sensitive presentation of such cultural subject matter. In our part of the country, Appalachian "hillbillies," Native Americans, and "Old South" types have all been targets of superficial, stereotyped, and romanticized depictions at tourist traps. At worst, such treatments can be grossly inaccurate and deeply offensive to the communities they purport to depict. At best they only reinforce cliched notions less discriminating tourists are likely to bring into a cultural encounter, or they obscure the realities of local and contemporary culture by dwelling on a storybook generic heritage.

Most importantly, today's serious cultural tourism consumers want a higher quality cultural experience, and they are willing to go far out of their way to have real encounters with real people who are different from them. On one hand, meeting this demand may be especially challenging because there is usually no organized local interest group ready to provide the means. Yet even communities who may consider themselves short on conventional historic or artistic resources may have an abundance of overlooked resources in their "folklife" or "folk culture," from tangible to intangible aspects of everyday life, including the ways people work and play, the things they do to their surroundings, their language and indigenous arts, often things they take for granted that others would find interesting. While the local bearers of a community's living heritage are not likely, particularly at first, to be assertive participants in tourism planning, folklorists and related cultural specialists can help assess what the community's "way of life" resources actually are and how they might be enlisted in tourism efforts.

There are doubtless some destinations that really don't want to go to the trouble of developing quality cultural tourism programs of the sort I'm describing, just as there inevitably are cultural attractions that don't live up to their advertising claims of authenticity and integrity. But the kinds of distinctions and standards I'm trying to suggest are nonetheless very important for the development and overall credibility of the cultural tourism industry. They need to be looked at in much greater detail, and the field needs to arrive at better common language and understandings about them. There are many reasons, for example, that a classification or ranking system for cultural tourism attractions and destinations might be of value. In recreational tourism, comparative ratings afford consumers of white water streams or hiking trails very reliable yardsticks about their character and difficulty, which then provide the basis for informed choices. At present, cultural and heritage tourism products are obviously quite diverse, and rigorous market study would probably reveal important differences among consumers as well. Until the field utilizes better standards and more insightful product and marketing information, it runs the risk not only of pursuing haphazard and inefficient development strategies, but also of earning a "buyer beware" reputation.

Recent success stories in our region point to the fact that unique and high-quality cultural tourism initiatives grow from honest appraisals of an area's cultural reality, and they pursue alternative themes that are specific to the place's heritage. In southeastern Tennessee, for example, the Tennessee Overhill project has rejected the conventional approaches to packaging southern Appalachian culture. Instead of joining the many other destinations where cultural attractions emphasize isolated and primitive mountain life of a pioneer past, the three counties of the Overhill have become one of the few places where visitors can witness and learn about the industrialization of the mountains. The theme followed from acknowledgment that it was the railroad, textile mills, and mining that really defined the identities of most communities in the area. Local museums and a driving tour now work together to interpret the visible history of company towns, worker housing, old machinery, and even environmental damage and recovery (Ballard 1991; Caldwell 1994; Ward 1994).

Root cultures do offer valuable tourism resources, but tourist attractions too often tend to repackage, fictionalize, or sanitize what they present, rather than bringing tourists in contact with root traditions that are still alive in host communities. In the Mississippi Delta, "blues tourism" has seen remarkable growth, in large part because the area's grassroots musicians and musical venues have been made so accessible to visitors. An area known for its poverty, the Delta has during the past decade capitalized on its musical heritage as the theme of a homegrown tourism campaign targeting blues fans worldwide. The Delta Blues Museum and the Sunflower River Blues Festiva in Clarksdale serve as focal points, but individual and group tourists now fan out across the countryside to such unlikely attractions small-town juke joints and sleepy crossroads, cemeteries, and abandoned plantation dwellings associated with the area's legendary blues figures. As added benefit, the tourism movement has enhanced the sense of local identity and pride, especially among African-American citizens, helping to spawn blues programs in community schools, affording new opportunities to local musicians, and attracting assistance and visits from musical celebrities (Pettus 1990; Bessman 1993; Wilkie 1994; O'Neal 1990).

Efforts sponsored by Tennessee State Parks have made root cultural resources accessible to tourists across the state, yet these accomplishments have gone largely unheralded in tourist development circles in part because they have so successfully served local community audiences as well. From 1979 to 1985, the Tennessee State Parks Folklife Project employed trained fieldworkers at over 20 state parks. These folklorists conducted documentary research in the surrounding areas to identify traditional artists and folk cultural resources for park programming. A wide array of festivals, performances, demonstrations, and interpretive exhibits resulted (Allen 1981; Belanus 1986). At about ten sites, annual events created or reshaped by the project, such as Old Timers' Day at Pickett State Park and The Mountaineer Folk Festival at Fall Creek Falls State Park, continue to enhance their areas' cultural tourism offerings. At N.B. Forrest State Park, project research produced The Tennessee River Folklife Center, one of the state's finest small museums which interprets the cultural heritage of commercial fishing, musselling, boatbuilding, and other waterways traditions in this part of the state (Fulcher 1986a). In Clay County, parks efforts have contributed to the revival of "Rolley Hole," a unique traditional marble game. The annual National Rolley Hole Marbles Tournament at Standing Stone State Park now enjoys a reputation as one of the most unusual local culture events in the South and attracts international visitors (Wick 1985; Wynne 1986; Fulcher 1986b; Cope 1992).

Locals and Outsiders

The premise of cultural diversity is important not only in thinking about the tourism product, but also in remaining aware that cultural tourism involves constantly managing situations of intercultural contact. If tourism development takes credit for the economic benefits of bringing in outside visitors, it must also bear responsibility for the other results and complications of visitation. Provisions for buffering cultural contact are important ingredients in the development plan, and they need to address both sides of the dynamic: that of the locals as well as that of the outsiders. Many factors may affect relations between the two, but tourist developers have typically addressed only those that concern the visitor. Outsiders bring with them all kinds of preconceptions, expectations, and behaviors, from "Deliverance" stereotypes that may underlie real reservations about dealing with some people in the community, to assumptions about using credit cards or getting liquor-by-the-drink, to culturally conditioned ways of speaking or transacting business. Tourism promoters want visitors to feel safe and happy, and they've conventionally tried to accommodate such matters through "hospitality training" for key people in the host community.

But locals may also have a range of reactions to outsiders, and good reasons for them. Tourists who are not good guests or intercultural negotiators may conduct themselves in condescending, prejudiced, or pushy ways. Poorly managed cultural tourism settings, defined with only the visitor in mind, may make locals feel like caged bears or subservient display items. My grandmother, a weaver in a Carolina mountain craft shop during the 1950s, sometimes confided to family members her reservations about being gawked at by "those women from Florida in tight britches and sunglasses." We attributed it to Meemaw's old-timey ways, but the more I do cultural programming, the more I realize that this is a recurrent problem that often makes the best living resource people hard to involve in such activities, and that bringing more sensitivity into presentations can do a good deal to overcome it.

As heritage tourism increasingly tries to bring visitors in contact with real local culture in real contexts, there is a danger of outsiders intruding too much on the everyday life of the community. Designated places and events will always be the focal points for tourist activity, and when that activity becomes especially intense, they take on the air of a cultural no-man's-land, especially among locals who may then tend to avoid them. Good programs will find ways to create special opportunities for outsiders to venture beyond the predictable settings and have less rehearsed encounters with local people. But there will be a fine line of privacy, which probably varies from one place to another and needs to be acknowledged and respected. Strangers are likely welcome in most places on Main Street or the square, or in public parks, but how about the local liar's bench or barbecue pit, flea markets and auctions, the stockyards, out-of-the-way general stores, country music barndances? How about stopping at farm houses in the county's boondocks or on the "wrong side of the tracks," dropping into religious services or roadhouse honky-tonks?

It's extremely important for a cultural tourism program to be concerned with managing diversity on the homefront as well, and this is best approached by involving as many elements of the community as possible in the planning process. If the objective is to cultivate the entire community's turf as a tourism product, a "members-only" input policy, which is all too often enlisted by chambers of commerce, has inherent flaws. Hotel, restaurant, commercial attraction, and retail tourism businesses obviously want such a venture to succeed, but they are almost guaranteed to meet resistance if they impose it on the community and seek public resources in doing so. Rethinking the local tourism constituency, and building a broader coalition of support, is essential to securing community consent and a first step toward building a healthy cultural tourism environment. It also means sharing power and benefits.

Most history and arts activists assume they'll have to "infiltrate" the tourism industry to gain a place at the planning table (Roddewig 1988). It would be much smarter for tourism developers to invite them, not only because they control valuable resources, but also because the boards and memberships of their local non-profit entities are inroads to community opinion and support. The tax-exempt status of historical societies and arts councils qualifies them to apply for matching grants from public humanities and arts agencies as well as other funding sources. Forming strong coalitions of local interests and addressing broad community needs, including those related to tourism, help to make such grant proposals successful. Other local entities, from extension office programs to civic clubs, offer comparable partnership potential.

Tapping a community's organized cultural presence is the easy part. Similarly involving the people who represent the root culture and cultural diversity of a locale may be much more difficult. They're less likely to be "joiners," to be in touch with development talk at the county seat, or to be convinced anybody really wants to hear what they think. These are the people who most need to be reached in thoroughly identifying cultural resources and getting to the ones not already recognized. If this job is done well, it will also secure other sorts of public input into the planning process, identifying themes and ideas about what really makes up the local heritage and how people in the community want it to be depicted, community concerns that need to be addressed about possible negative affects of tourism; and prospective goals and incentives which, if met, would help assure a sense of community ownership of the tourism effort. This degree of assessment and input requires a real commitment to planning, but it is the only reliable way to take the community pulse regarding cultural tourism issues (for discussion of such a local effort sponsored by the National Park Service, see Hufford 1993).

Tourism developers, and sometimes history or arts advocates, may need to be convinced that professional consultation is important to this process. The suggestion that "it sounds like a fun job for someone local" underestimates what has to be accomplished, the expertise and skills required to do it, and the mediator's role associated with the job. An individual with training in folklore or a related field knows how to go about conducting an inventory of a community's cultural traditions and the people who sustain them, and they have the interview and documentation experience necessary to produce effective results. Nonprofessionals often trivialize the fundamentals of cultural diversity and show patronizing or condescending approaches to it. The cultural specialist, a neutral outsider without attachment to the local social order, can more efficiently establish rapport with and earn the trust of diverse people in the community.

In communities where few previous efforts have tried to span cultural differences, the work of the cultural specialist may become a lightning rod for these issues. In feeling out matters of community involvement and public relations for tourism, they may turn up controversial points that have simply been ignored in the past. From a management perspective, it's far better to find out about such things at the planning stage, and to seek ways to deal with them diplomatically then, than to be blindsided by them when a new wave of tourists arrives. The cultural specialist's job, in addition to identifying community resources, is not simply to manipulate public opinion in favor of tourism development, and there are no guarantees of unanimous community support. Some dissent can probably be expected, and allowing the cultural specialist to occupy middle ground can mean the difference between trying to reconcile dissent in good faith and turning a deaf ear to it.

Scrutinizing all a community's culture against the prospects of tourism puts an immediacy to the most basic question of whether the community actually does want to encourage cultural tourism. The reactions—from enthusiasm to apathy to misgivings—will encompass both the predictable and the surprising. Some element of the local elite may object to involving cultural subject matter that does not, in their mind, support a flattering or progressive local image. Some business interests may feel threatened by the prospect of broadening the scope of local attractions. Adamant supporters may hold unachievable expectations. But it has to be understood that assessing resources and asking the question is only the starting point for planning. The process of balancing conflicting visions against common interests, and working through questions of scale and emphasis, takes time. Involving community input is a commitment to a gradual, long-range, and ultimately realistic strategy for tourist development (Lane 1994).

Preparing, Promoting, and Preserving

After the fact-finding, many decisions need to be made about priorities—which needs should be addressed first and which should wait—and about how additional cultural resources can be brought into the tourism development scheme. Professional input remains important to assure quality in the ways local culture is interpreted and presented. Efforts that are poorly conceived or produced will not result in creditable tourism products. Involving expertise in most cases also proves cost-effective, leading to informed decisions about how to make the most out of limited budgets.

Specific improvements should contribute to the long-term goal of enhancing representations of local culture in places and events where tourists are desired. Museums and information centers are focal points for visitation, and they should contain a clear overview of the local cultural story, covering themes and topics visitors will encounter in the community. Content here, as in all exhibits, brochures, guides, and other interpretive materials, should contain good general explanations balanced with concrete local references or illustrations. Exhaustive displays of collections, uncaptioned photographs, and disorganized "show-and-tell" often detract from the goal of interpretation.

There are many creative ways to develop interpretive aids for visitors that will help them understand and appreciate what they experience as they move from a facility into the wider community. Walking and driving tours are now familiar cultural tourism devices. Careful planning of their maps and suggested routes can influence where visitors go—and don't go—in the community, and unlike museums, they're not limited to "open hours." Conventional tours too often concentrate only on landmarks and homes of the famous, missing opportunities to satisfy outsiders' curiosity about other things they might see, or to point out characteristics of vernacular life so common that locals take them for granted. Examples include cemetery practices, building types, traditional varieties of gardening or yard ornamentation, sites where typical occupational or agricultural activity takes place, features that illustrate how local people relate to aspects of the natural environment, or other tangible evidence of local customs. Such elements all contribute to the overall sense of place, and visitors may be surprisingly fascinated by them if they are given adequate information in brochure text or signage.

Bringing the human dimension into interpretation is very effective. It seems trite, but tourists love to hear people speak the local dialect. Interpretation should incorporate opportunities for them to do so, as long as care is taken to avoid it being done in ways that are either "put on" or demeaning. Local guides—people willing to talk with and answer questions from tourists about the community or what they do—are extremely valuable resources. Identifying people with potential and getting them involved in special tours or tour stops may take time and diplomacy. Local businesses might afford occasional tours as a way of supporting the tourism effort. For some situations, such as taking visitors off the normal tourist beat, it would be useful to have a group of local independent paid guides who could be called upon for specialty tours and activities.

On the Natchez Trace Parkway in Hickman County, the National Park Service has involved the active cultural landscape and the human element in an especially innovative interpretive site, where visitors can stop in on a working tobacco farm. If nobody's around, the exhibit modules next to the patch and inside the barn explain the basics about growing tobacco, while the farmer, Billy Coleman of Duck River, tells them about the cycle of seasonal work by way of a button-activated recording . If they happen to be there on the right day or time of year, tourists can talk to Coleman or his helpers while they work the crop, or they might experience the sight and smell of housed burley. But regardless of its timing, the stop affords informative, first-hand contact with a particular sort of farming as it is typically practiced in the area.

The variables of time and space, as well as other considerations, often make it difficult for visitors to witness local culture in context. Events, where activities can be staged for tourist consumption, offer another programming possibility. In many communities, annual festivals already muster joint energies to attract tourism and include some elements of cultural presentation. Improving such an event is a likely priority in cultural tourism development, and that task involves working with the living bearers of local cultural traditions, including folk music and dance performers, indigenous craftspeople, and individuals who practice similar folkways.

The easiest people to "book" for festivals and other live programming—like schooled musicians who interpret folk songs, choreographed dance troupes who perform to recorded music, or studio craftspeople accustomed to the craft fair circuit—are often not particularly authentic to local traditions. There are many ins and outs to presenting folk artists well, starting, once again, with identifying these resources. It takes advance time and patient diplomacy to cultivate such people, a determination to bridge cultural differences, and sensitivity to their point of view. Some who are unaccustomed to promoting themselves may not be able to demonstrate or participate without special assistance. Good interpretation remains important at festivals, concerts, demonstrations, and similar live events. Informative and respectful introductions of folk artists not only improve their audience's experience, they help make the artists feel good about what they're doing and more likely to want to do other public programs (Cauthen 1994; Cogswell 1991; Wilson and Udall 1982).

In relating to grassroots artists, tourist development efforts are especially likely to touch on conflicts between commercial orientations and the goal of appropriately showcasing the local "way of life." In festivals, fundraising aspects should not be confused with interpretive programming. As state folklorist, I sometimes refer festival organizers to good folk artists in their area. More than once I've been embarrassed to find out that artists invited to demonstrate at my suggestion were then expected to pay to do so, even when they had nothing to sell. In general, participants asked to perform or actively demonstrate at an event (as opposed to just selling) should themselves be paid at least a modest honorarium for doing so. The idea that an appearance is a promotional opportunity for the artist, justifying unpaid participation, is not valid, and such event-management policies are guaranteed to alienate potential participants.

Really getting to know a community's cultural resources requires considerable familiarity with grassroots artists and craftspeople, and smart development efforts will make them feel invested by trying hard to fairly address their circumstances and concerns. There are many myths and complications involved in promotion and marketing of folk art and other local artwork. Development strategies often assume or claim far more benefits to traditional artists than entrepreneurial or poorly-planned sales arrangements actually produce (Cogswell 1992). Local markets, in fact, usually have limited profit potential, and the competition can create diplomatic quicksand for community-wide efforts, especially when they play favorites with particular artists or retailers. Sales cooperatives have many advantages, but they take great effort to organize and run smoothly (*Cooperative Approach* 1985). Documenting economic activity in this area may pose problems, as it is likely to overlap with the community's off-the-books cash economy. Elderly and low-income artists may be deterred or otherwise affected by the supplemental income ceilings of social support programs. Grassroots artists whose work may be very saleable in other places are often taken advantage of as outside interests become active in the local market (Draper 1991; Cogswell 1992:214–15). Local artists may not need sales opportunities, at least at first, as much as they need technical assistance aimed at the business and practical aspects of marketing their work, like self-promotion, pricing, negotiating, taxes and other legalities (Wells 1989). By addressing that need, the tourism development strategy can help prepare this constituency for tourism opportunities and help extend real economic benefits to a broader community base.

In Cannon County, the chair- and basket-making capital of Tennessee, a model project aimed at showcasing the local craft legacy and stimulating sales to tourists illustrates a good initial approach to working with a community of artisans. The product was a published directory of the county's folk artists and craftsmen, giving information about all the individuals who wanted to participate: what they made, where they lived, comments on their work, and contact information (*Cannon County* 1987). An introduction and photographs gave interpretive quality to the booklet, and maps and directions added elements of a tour brochure. Availability was made known in periodicals read by serious craft buyers, and the booklet was actually sold, with proceeds earmarked to print future revisions. Quite aside from actual craft sales, the project was most successful as an organizing point for the craft community. It got them thinking for the first time about common interests and tourism potential. It led to marketing workshops, an annual craft fair, exhibits, and a craft presence at a new local arts center. To me, it's always illustrated the importance of getting off on the right foot.

As a promotion, the booklet's targeted distribution also illustrates a good point about linking cultural resources to specific sorts of tourism consumers. Cultural tourists inclined to out-of-the-way places may, as a whole, tend to cut against the normal tourism grain, and mainstream marketing strategies—like hosting travel-writers' tours and buying big-ticket advertising—may not be the most effective way to reach some of the most likely visitors. One aspect of assessing a community's cultural resources is trying to identify "alternative" tourists predisposed to an interest in them. The successful connections of blues fans with the Mississippi Delta and marble enthusiasts with the National Rolley Hole Tournament have already been mentioned. Another example is the devotees of alternative medicine who are now drawn to the Folk Medicine Festival that celebrates the tradition of healing waters in Red Boiling Springs (Cope 1994). Such interest groups are not only especially appreciative of the resource-attraction, and of local efforts to interpret or present it, but they also have high potential to be return tourists. Their newsletters, magazines, and networks offer excellent possibilities for targeted marketing. In 1989, our Folk Arts Program at the Tennessee Arts Commission published a guide to the state's thirty fiddle contests, most local affairs with very limited advertising, and then mailed them out in response to requests following publicity in bluegrass and old-time music publications nationwide (Cogswell 1989). I'm sure most of the copies picked up at welcome center racks were thrown away, but the ones mailed to out-of-state musicians and fans hit the bullseye. I still regularly hear from people who have seen a copy and want to know about and visit these Tennessee events.

The goal of long-range development strategies is to continually strengthen a community's overall cultural tourism environment, and this includes looking after the health of the cultural resources that provide its foundation. More short-sighted approaches to seizing cultural tourism opportunities may risk "killing the goose that lays the golden egg." The protection of heritage resources is a fairly recent concern, and history activitists have been particularly effective in raising public consciousness about it, in part because the resources and results of historic preservation are so clearly observable in the physical environment. We can see and touch old buildings, and experiencing their presence or loss constantly reminds us of their value, the costs of neglect, and the rewards of preservation. It's been fairly easy to establish consensus about what's destructive and what's good for these resources, and public policies and programs to encourage preservation have followed.

Much of what I've referred to as "way of life," is not nearly so concrete, but it is nonetheless real: what people know, think, and value; how they work and play, speak and create. In the concern for this wider scope of culture and heritage, "cultural intangibles" is the term being applied to such things. Broadening and including the approach of historic preservation, "cultural conservation" is the objective of protecting all cultural resources. It is a relatively new and complex goal, but there has already been a great deal of interest in establishing the principles, guidelines, policies, and practical strategies by which it can be achieved (Loomis 1983; Howell 1988; Feintuch 1988: Baron and Spitzer 1992). A romantic layman's view may regard most cultural intangibles as comparable to "dying arts," doomed to extinction, and the cause of cultural conservation therefore as a futile one. But it's not that simple. Elements of culture do change, yet there remain, in cultures of place and ethnicity, characteristics that continue and evolve over time, serving as keys to identity. And in modern times, those characteristics are increasingly intangible. Heritage is a dynamic thing, and cultural conservation is more than just hanging on to relics of the past. It seeks ways to allow individual cultures to stay vital and different cultures to remain diverse. How does all this relate to tourism strategies and programming? It underscores that tourism development will have effects on local cultures, as regarded in the widest possible sense. If planners are serious about marketing the local heritage as a tourism product, it is in their best interest to consider in detail and try to control what those effects might be. Thinking about cultural conservation issues during the planning process will bring alternatives to the table which deserve to be considered as priorities are set and decisions are made. Making sure that the planning process is not oblivious or resistant to the possibility of damaging cultural effects is a good start in avoiding them. Honesty in evaluating programs and willingness to adjust them in this respect are also important. Pro-active stances on cultural conservation are best of all; that is, trying to assist or stimulate cultural traditions as part of development objectives. Many well-designed programs may contain an element of this, but it needs to be more than lip-service. Rather than just showing off the heritage to tourists, programs should also aspire to increase local interest and pride in unique traditions, create situations where traditional skills can be passed on, or provide other real help where it's needed.

Opportunities to put cultural conservation principles into action depend largely on local circumstances, but only by keeping such things in mind will the opportunities be recognized. Two examples from other parts of the Southeast illustrate how wide-ranging such opportunities might be. Generations of tourists visiting the South Carolina lowlands have purchased coiled sweetgrass baskets in the Charleston Market and the Mount Pleasant area, but the African-American women who make them have faced increasing difficulty in securing their traditional materials. As resorts proliferate on the coast, new land owners have denied them access to dunes where the grasses grow, and they've had to drive for hours into Georgia and Florida to harvest what they need. A consortium of regional interests finally helped them seek solutions; they have now secured rights to harvest co-operatively from designated local areas and, with assistance from agricultural experts, have started a program to cultivate their own sweetgrass patches. A highway development project has also imperiled the independent roadside stands where rural makers have always sold their work, and negotiations are now pursuing compromise plans that would permit the ladies to continue to sell in their traditional way (*Proceedings* 1988; Rosengarten 1992). In both instances, innovative accommodations will help conserve one of the state's most important cultural tourism resources.

Tourism planners in Eunice, Louisiana, faced many decisions about the sensitive presentation of Cajun culture to outsiders. As one of the cornerstones of local programming, they initiated a Saturday night concert series in a restored theater to feature regional Cajun and Zydeco music groups. Tourism consultants insisted that all the shows' introductions and announcements should be done in English so that the visitors they hoped to attract could understand. Local cultural advocates objected, and after controversy, the first show was presented in Cajun French. This arrangement prevailed when it proved to be a point of pride, assuring both a community sense of ownership for the event and attendance by locals. Tourists enjoyed it as a much more authentic experience, and it encouraged their interaction with locals to get translations (Ancelet 1992).

The outcome in Eunice also nicely illustrates a final point. Just as it's appropriate to broaden the idea of local constituencies for planning in cultural tourism, there is room as well for more alternative thinking about consumers and audiences. Conventional tourism marketing seems to emphasize reaching out-of-staters, over-nighters, and big-time spenders. The point of a long-term strategy is that it takes time to finetune a quality cultural tourism destination, and alternative venues, especially those trying to build a tourism reputation from scratch or remold one, can't afford to ignore matters closer to home. Locals won't bring in new money, but they are an audience for tourism attractions, even if the attractions are built around them. Their enthusiasm for what's happening in the community can influence day visitors from surrounding areas, and more attention to this market also helps build a broader base.

A development strategy that's well-rounded will address many components and levels, and investments of planning time, energy, and money should reflect that. The expenditure of local bed tax revenues is probably the best index of real tourism development priorities. If it all goes into advertising, the local industry is not taking other aspects of development very seriously. Earmarking some of that money for local cultural interpretation and programming will not only improve the tourism product, but also demonstrate industry commitment to a real partnership with the community in the business of cultural tourism.

References

Abney, George (1994) "Going National." *Historic Preservation News*, August/September, 20–21, 26.

Allen, Ray (1981) "The Use of State and Local Parks in Folklife Programming." *Tennessee Folklore Society Bulletin* 47 (December):160–4.

Ancelet, Barry Jean (1992) "Cultural Tourism in Cajun Land: Shotgun Wedding or Marriage Made in Heaven?" *Southern Folklore* 49:263–4.

Arnow, Pat (1991) "Tourist Central: Scourge or Salvation?," *Now and Then* 8(1):6–13.

Ballard, Sandra L. (1991) "Tennessee's Overhill Country: Preserving the Industrial Revolution." *Now and Then* 8(1):24–7.

Baron, Robert and Nicholas R. Spitzer (1992) *Public Folklore*. Washington, DC: Smithsonian Institution Press.

Belanus, Betty J. (1986) "Fieldwork in Public Sector Folklore: The Tennessee State Parks Folklife Example." *Tennessee Folklore Society Bulletin* 52 (Spring):6–10.

Bessman, Jim (1993) "Ever-Growing Delta Blues Museum Keeps Music's History Alive." *Billboard*, 4 December, 16, 48.

Caldwell, Linda (1994) "Creating a New Community." *Touchstone: The Magazine of the Tennessee Humanities Council* 26:8–12.

Cannon County Folk Artists & Craftsmen: A Directory (1987) Woodbury, TN: Cannon County Rural Area Development Committee.

Cauthen, Joyce (1994) *Presenting Mississippi's Traditional Artists: A Handbook for*

Local Arts Agencies. Jackson: Mississippi Arts Commission.

Cogswell, Robert, ed. (1989) *Fiddle and Old-Time Music Contests in Tennessee.* Nashville: Folk Arts Program, Tennessee Arts Commission.

Cogswell, Robert (1991) "Folk Artists as Tourism Resources." *Tennessee Folklore Society Bulletin* 55:26–9.

Cogswell, Robert (1992) "Cultural Intervention in Southern Appalachia: Agents and Agendas." *Southern Folklore* 49:212–15.

The Cooperative Approach to Crafts (1985) Agricultural Cooperative Service Information Report 33. Washington, DC: United State Department of Agriculture.

Cope, Cathleen (1992) "The Rolley Holers." *Tennessee Magazine* 36:9 (September):7–10.

Cope, Cathleen (1994) "Folk Medicine Festival." *Tennessee Magazine* 38:7 (July):16–19.

De Kadt, Emanuel, ed. (1979) *Tourism: Passport to Development?* London: Oxford University Press.

Draper, Robert (1991) "Plunder or Patronage?" *American Way (American Airlines Flight Magazine)* 24(10):16ff.

Fedarko, Kevin (1993) "Miami's Tourist Trap." *Time,* 20 September, 71.

Feintuch, Burt, ed. (1988) *The Conservation of Culture: Folklore and the Public Sector.* Lexington: University Press of Kentucky.

Fletcher, Martin (1993) "Egypt—Is This the Time to Visit?" *Travel & Leisure,* June, 60ff.

Fromer, Arthur (1988) "Historic Preservation and Tourism," *Preservation Forum,* Fall, 10–12.

Fulcher, Bobby (1986a) "Pilot Knob: The Tennessee River Folklife Center." *Tennessee Conservationist* 52:1 (January/February):4–6.

Fulcher, Robert J. (1986b) "Rolley Hole Marbles." *1986 Festival of American Folklife Program.* Washington, DC: Smithsonian Institution, 56–60.

"Getting Started: How to Succeed in Heritage Tourism" (1993) Washington, DC: National Trust for Historic Preservation.

Gubernick, Lisa (1993) "Damage Control." *Forbes,* 19 July, 196ff.

Howell, Benita J. ed. (1988) *Cultural Heritage Conservation in the American South.* Southern Anthropological Society Proceedings 23. Athens: University of Georgia Press.

Hufford, Mary (1993) "Breaking the Time Barrier: Folklife and Heritage Planning in Southern West Virginia." *Folklife Center News* 15(3–4):3–23.

Humphrey, Tom (1989) "Study: Sevier Pays a Price for Tourism." *Knoxville News-Sentinel,* 16 March.

Lane, Pat (1994) "Cultural Tourism—A Long-Term Strategy for Community Development. An Interview with Benita Howell." *Touchstone: The Magazine of the Tennessee Humanities Council* 26:3–7.

"Looking Forward: The National Trust Program Council Report" (1988) *Preservation Forum,* Fall, 13–16.

Loomis, Ormond H. (1983) *Cultural Conservation: The Protection of Cultural Heritage in the United States*. Washington: Library of Congress.

Moskin, Bill and Sandy Guettler (1988) *Setting the Stage: Practical Guide to Building Arts & Tourism Partnerships in the Californias*. Sacramento: California Arts Council and California Office of Tourism.

O'Neal, Jim (1990) "A Traveler's Guide to the Crossroads." *Living Blues* 94 (November/December):21–4

Pettus, Gary (1990) "Explosion in the Delta." *The (Jackson, MS) Clarion-Ledger*, 10 August, 1Eff.

Powers, Ron (1986) *White Town Drowsing: Journeys to Hannibal*. Boston: Atlantic Monthly Press.

Proceedings of the Sweetgrass Basket Conference (1988) Columbia, SC: South Carolina Folk Arts Program, McKissick Museum, University of South Carolina.

Roddewig, Richard J. (1988) "Selling America's Heritage—Without Selling Out." *Preservation Forum*, Fall, 2.

Rosengarten, Dale (1992) "Lowcountry Basketry: Folk Arts in the Marketplace." *Southern Folklore* 49:240–55.

Smith, Michael (1989) *Behind the Glitter: The Impact of Tourism on Rural Women in the Southeast*. Lexington: Southeast Women's Employment Coalition.

Smith, Valene L., ed. (1989) *Hosts and Guests, The Anthropology of Tourism*. Philadelphia: University of Pennsylvania Press.

Smith, Valene L. and William R. Eadington, eds (1992) *Tourism Alternatives: Potentials and Problems in the Development of Tourism*. Philadelphia: University of Pennsylvania Press.

"Staying Away: Egypt" (1994) *The Economist*, 19 February, 45ff.

Stoker, Melissa (1993) "Crime Takes a Bite Out of Local Tourism" *Orlando Business Journal*, 24 September, 4ff.

Ward, James A. (1994) "Around the Historic Overhill." *Touchstone: The Magazine of the Tennessee Humanities Council* 26:13–16.

Wells, Patricia A. (1989) *Handbook for Tennessee Folk Artists*. Nashville: Folk Arts Program, Tennessee Arts Commission.

"When Taming is Inflaming" (1992) *The Economist*, 19 December, 41.

Wick, Don (1985) "Marble Marvels of the Hill Country." *Ford Times*, February, 26ff.

Wiener, Jon (1994) "Tall Tales and True." *The Nation*, 31 January, 133–6.

Wilkie, Curtis (1994) "Blues Get Devotion in Delta." *The Boston Globe*, 15 February.

Wilson, Joe and Lee Udall (1982) *Folk Festivals: A Handbook for Organization and Management*. Knoxville: University of Tennessee Press.

Wynne, Joe (1986) "Rolley Hole!" *Tennessee Conservationist* 52:1 (January/February):7–9.

2

THE MARKETING OF ABORIGINAL AUSTRALIA: RITUAL, REALITY, AND REVELATION

KEITH HOLLINSHEAD

Introduction

The pronounced global trend away from acquisitive travel to experiential travel and the sudden immensity of Australia's late appeal as a safe and varied vacationland has recently placed the market spotlight on the presentation and interpretation of "Black Australia" as one of the new tourism products of our age (Altman 1989). Aboriginal Australia is being stirred from its longtime torpor to its first blush of limelight on the international stage. The marketing fellowship sees outback Australia as a novel and wide playground in the traveling public's emergent and energetic quest for cultural authenticity. As "Black Australia" is being brought within the grasp of the imagination of our contemporary adventure-seeking and world-conquering tourists, crucial challenges are being placed before the industries' marketing power-brokers and playmakers. Have they in the boardrooms of Australia [and beyond] their own necessary imagination to do the job? Are they up to the task of promoting and yet preserving the ancient indigenous "Dreamtime?" In many respects these Australian marketeers walk an ecological and cultural tightrope (Altman and Finlayson 1991). They will, hereafter, as is commonly said of the nation herself, be judged by the way they treat "their aborigines." This chapter will show that the major challenge is one of perception. Too many individuals who work in the industry "downunder" view Aboriginal society as backward and meager. There is insufficient respect for Aboriginal culture, and a tendency within the industry to trivialize the stories of the Dreamtime when they are known (Hollinshead 1996). Initially and vitally, the continuing significance of the land for Aboriginal people needs to be appreciated. Its intrinsic association with Black identity via collective myth, history and custodianship needs to be valued. That careful custodianship is destined to become increasingly controversial as the sub-continent of "Northern Australia" is promoted to become a major international tourist destination and different mining, grazing and governmental interests endeavor to deny Aboriginal rights.

In some ways, therefore, it is not surprising to learn that many Aboriginal groups actually welcome the tourist invasion. Indeed, one estimation now suggests that at the time of press there are as many as 150 "Aboriginal owned and run" tourism operations across Australia (Borton-Taylor 1996). Their entry into tourism is perhaps unavoidable, but it is not necessarily undesirable on their part. Many Aborigines clearly see it both as a novel way of safeguarding their physical patrimony and consolidating their social community. Their own principal effort now is to prevent any modern-day bonding to the powerbrokers of tourism where those playmakers in the industry are representative of a new malign neo-colonial force. The welcomed advance of tourism toward the sacred sites of Aboriginal people is perhaps, for them, a new move in the old pursuit of "hanging on" to save lore, land and life. Above all, therefore, aboriginal groups and communities must be encouraged and enabled by the industry itself to prevent rape of the culture by external ignorance. Whilst the marketing fellowship must learn to understand, the Aboriginal people must learn to be understood.

Developing Areas

In terms of its geographical location vis-à-vis existing mainstream tourism thoroughfares and of the cultural appeal that is "the outback," Aboriginal Australia can be regarded as still very much a "developing country," albeit by some "a third world nation within a nation." It is therefore important that the general issues facing developing regions are examined before the individual features of that society are explored.

A number of factors have fired the expansion of worldwide experiential travel, such as improved transportation, advanced communication, educational enlightenment, and an easing of psychological mobility for the world's traveling public (Lundberg 1985:125). Indeed one principal commentator considers that the form and movement of travel has been so comprehensively measured that tourism may indeed be "the best-researched single topic in history" (Smith 1977:1). That does not necessarily mean, in her view, that the research has either been sufficient or precise, nor even that the correct conclusions have been drawn from it for any given emergent area. Indeed, other observers consider tourism to be far from an easy industry for developing countries or Third World areas to enter:

> The mass tourist is not interested in the problems faced by the host country. He [*sic!*] has invested a lot of money into his holiday and he does not want to experience bureaucratic red tape, unfamiliar food, inadequate nightlife, badly designed hotels or untrained waiters. The destination countries have therefore to get all these aspects of a holiday very quickly right, if their resorts are going to survive in the increasing competitive world of international tourism. It means the planners have got to know the tourist very well... (Turner and Ash 1975:125).

Tourism, however, is rarely a neutral "innocent" activity, and its impacts have been proven to be capable of being "divisive, far-reaching and long-term ... nothing less than the rewriting of the economic and political geography of the world" (ibid.). The principal danger is that when a given tourism region is managed by outsiders it can become a form of "imperialism," and for the host population a form of neo-colonialism (Nash 1977:33). The original appeal of the region may have been the pursuit of the simple or the primitive, where the metropolitan traveler seeks pre-industrial culture, and searches for the antiquated, the ethnic and the pristine. The problem is that such isolated or removed cultures can only retain their untarnished individuality if their remoteness and sanctity are preserved, and yet such external presentations of indigenous peoples can amount to unthinking forms of "othering" where that target population is subjugated or objectified by the industry as an unchanging people incapable of becoming contemporary (Hollinshead and De Burlo, in press). Elsewhere, in so many other peripheral locations, the provision of a new international tourist resort has been almost immediately accompanied by the appearance of some of the grossest features of metropolitan culture. In the South Pacific, for instance, the economic impact of these new leisure tastes and expenditure patterns has been catastrophic for host communities whose traditional social structures were non-monetary:

> The dollar, the pound and the yen could turn out to be, in their different ways, quite as destructive as the syphilis and the tuberculosis that decimated the region's population in the eighteenth century (Turner and Ash 1975:165).

Thus tourism has the potential to intrude, and, for open or unsophisticated societies, it can convert the moral nexus into a cash one through both conscious and unconscious forms of othering committed by external travel marketeers and tourism planners (Hollinshead and De Burlo, in press). So-called "primitive" societies find it difficult to maintain group cohesion in the disruption, conflict, and stress that are so often the result of unchecked tourism and development. The pace of tourism becomes so alacrid and its shape so inflated that it moves beyond the sphere of community control.

While tourism is not inherently culturally damaging, it can indeed become so for a host population where its development is administered by exogenous forces over which that host society has reducing control. The critical issue appears to be *who is in charge of marketing management*, as Margaret Byrne Swain showed for the Cuna Indians of Panama (Swain 1977:71). In bringing the culture or the society "to the market," multinational companies, national enterprises, and regional governments must be encouraged to adopt more routinely "social marketing" perspectives or "relationship marketing" outlooks and consider carefully the benefits that accrue to the host population *as well as to* the various target visitor segments. The contemporary dilemma is all too often one of a mutual failure in understanding. Thus the disinclination of marketing agencies to become acquainted with the host community tends to be reciprocated by that local population's own accumulated bewilderment about tourism in general and about the particular integrated complexity of the industry's component parts.

Research in the last two decades appears to indicate that the best solution for this exploitative scenario is for marketing forces to help the local population themselves control the rate and form of the culture change that is induced by tourism (Butler and Hinch 1996). Thus, instead of being manipulated, the host population "manipulates itself." Cultural tourism can evolve into an "identity maintenance mechanism" (Hall 1996:161) which has real effect and symbolic power for group cohesion. There is, therefore, no inevitability in the process of tourist development, nor formulaic answers to ensure that a given region will be promoted profitably in the eyes of external entrepreneurs or appropriately from the perspective of the developing society (Selwyn 1996). If parasitic (and thereby myopic) tourism is to be denied, those responsible for the marketing effort must work with care at both their *science* (i.e., understanding the nature of the fit between the right benefit-seeking travelers and the resources of the given region) and their *art* (i.e., understanding how to enable and empower the host community to display faithfully and yet maintain its authentic cultural entities). If parasitic/myopic tourism is to be avoided, travel marketeers and tourism planners must work concertedly—or must be encouraged to work concertedly—to recognize and admit the very powerful and subjectifying ethnocentrisms by which they currently tend to work (Hollinshead 1993a,b).

Development of Aboriginal Tourism

Having clarified contemporary thought on tourism research for the generic problem of developing areas, I now turn to "Australian" Aborigines per se. A number of important background perspectives need to be made clear.

First, the poverty of the regard and level of awareness of Euraustralians for Aboriginal values must be recognized (Hollinshead 1996:335–345). While the two hundred years of Australia's supposed "Nationhood" has been a time of continual struggle by the Aborigines against many authorities and numerous institutions, it is only relatively recently that Euraustralians in any number have come to appreciate the wealth and vitality of the original inhabitants' culture. Indeed a typical Euraustralian view appears to have been that of the South Australian Protector of Aborigines in 1909:

> The white blood, being the strongest must in the end prevail ... and from this it is evident that the ultimate end of the Australian Aboriginal is to be merged with the general population, consequently the sooner they are physically and normally improved the better for the white race (Quoted in Toyne and Vachon 1984:21).

Thus so many Euraustralians have continually failed to view Black Australians from their own (Aboriginal) perspective. The marginal status of Black Australians in Australia is evident in the fact that they were first included in the national census by the referendum of 1967—a scant three decades ago (Department of the Chief Minister of the Northern Territory 1984:18). Thus the Euraustralian view of Aboriginal people has not for the most part been empathetic. Accordingly, the literature on the impact of tourism upon Aboriginal people is still in its infancy since "more has been written upon the effects of tourists upon inanimate objects such as rock art than upon the human descendants of those who created it" (Brady 1985:11). Today many of the principal Aboriginal features that might inspire tourist interest are claimed as being "Australian." Chief among them is Ayers Rock, now a veritable symbol of Australia itself and "part of white men's dreaming too" (Toyne and Vachon 1984:134).

Second, the response of Aboriginal people to the presence of Euraustralian institutions needs to be comprehended (Ross 1991). All too often non-Aboriginals write and think as though there is a single unified Aboriginal outlook or a single form of black behavior (Reynolds 1981:2). In fact the Aboriginal response to Euraustralian phenomena like tourism is generally much more varied and complex than most observers expect. On the one hand there are Aborigines who wish to distance themselves from tourists as they do for most, if not all, manifestations of Western society. They are attracted to the fecundity of the land and their predeliction is for residence on their own isolated outstations (Lawrence 1985:88). There are also Aborigines who accept tourism as a *fait accompli*, a fact of life. Such groups adapt to the presence of tourists just as they did to the presence of crocodile hunters, buffalo shooters and miners (Palmer 1985:9). Sometimes, moreover, the degree of support for tourism can be substantive even amongst the most traditionally minded Aboriginal people. Accordingly, Robert Layton makes clear that "there is no evidence to suggest that [at Ayers Rock in central Australia] the men saw any conflict between the existence of a National Park and their own traditional rights to the area," nor did they "want the [new resort of] Yulara to be separated in any way from Uluru [Ayers Rock] or Katatjuta [The Olgas]" (Layton 1986:98).

An important third point regarding the contemporary context of tourist visits to Aboriginal sites in Australia is that so few operators have as yet "bitten the bullet" on the concept. Whatever the nature of the expectation of visitor contact with Aboriginal culture:

> ...the reality is almost certainly a bone shattering disillusionment. With few exceptions the opportunity for visitors to experience or learn of Aboriginal culture is practically non-existent. Worse, those responsible for the delivery of tourist services are practically totally ignorant of the culture or captive of an ideological viewpoint which, as a result of other social experiences, is hostile and critical of that culture (Ellis 1984:74).

Thus the worldwide growth in adventure travel is derived for Australia (as for other vast regions with primeval landscapes) from what Francine de Plessix Gray referred to as the tourists' "impulse to restore innocence on the planet we have despoiled, a fantasy of returning to some non-violent state of nature" (Gray 1973:28). Yet the tourist industry in Australia does not appear to be geared up to either identify or interpret those "impulses" through the medium of Aboriginal culture, no matter how rich the product itself is (Horne 1992). The industry, it appears, is immature and suffers from a shortfall of imaginative capability.

The Propositions

While it is important that the social, economic and environmental impacts of tourism for a given developing region are comprehensively monitored, there is a danger that the responsible federal or state government can become unduly pessimistic about the overall impact of tourism (Cater 1987:220). The choice for Aboriginal Australia lies somewhere between two extremes. At one end of the scale, government agencies can frustrate the development of tourism in and among Aboriginal communities by helping to ensure that the majority of Aboriginal settlements remain true to traditional lifestyle in the guise of what Ellis styles "a personal, small scale society, jealous of privacy and cautious in its contact with outsiders" (Turner and Ash 1975:186). Alternatively, tourism can be permitted to rage rampant, corrupting "such frail elites by dangling a model of advanced western consumer society before their eyes" (ibid.). Such are *the dialectics* of tourism development for, with, and among indigenous populations— something which tourism researchers only very rarely probe (Hall 1994).

The collective role of marketing decision-makers in travel and tourism is to find an acceptable balance between those two points where *the scale* of tourism development is adapted to suit the cultural and resource realities of *each* local situation. To achieve this it is imperative that those responsible for marketing decisions forge healthy relationships with traditional and emergent Aboriginal groups. The tourism industry must above all else "listen." It must avoid at all costs the rancor of false and insincere negotiation, and reject the kind of "company-inspired public relations exercises" that the mining industry has all too frequently conducted at the expense of Aboriginal interests in Australia (Toyne and Vachon 1984:189). No amount of profitability from tourist visits could compensate Aboriginal groups and communities, for instance, for the Argyle Diamond Mine's desecration in mining of its newly possessed Barrimundi dreaming site. What is required to prevent such things happening within tourism is the provision of good market information supported by good marketing sense. This is the key to appropriate planning and decision-making with, and on behalf of, Aboriginal groups. A number of propositions are now offered, to help further compose the frame of reference that such operators and practitioners should take in helping promote Aboriginal "Australia."

Proposition 1: Creative Interpretation

Visitors' appreciation of aboriginal culture and cultural values is likely to be influenced by the quality of on-site interpretation

Visitors need a developed sense of awareness and insight to appreciate any cultural or heritage setting (Horne 1992); visitors *particularly* need a highly developed sense of imagination to enjoy a trip to most Aboriginal sites. Aboriginal people have not built arresting buildings which overtly and immediately take one's eye. Indeed, "The highest monuments built during the aboriginal epoch were heaps of empty shells [the shell middens]... of the Victoria coast" (Blainey 1976:138). It is conceivable, therefore, that the mythology of the Aboriginal "Dreamtime" stories and legends will best prove to offer the kind of new or authentic experience so increasingly sought after by travelers today. The telling of such stories and the packaging of such interpretation is, however, highly demanding. One of the weakest aspects of current tourism promotions for art sites at Kakadu and Uluru in the Northern Territory is that tours are generally led by guides "unfamiliar with the art" (Gale and Jacobs 1986:8). At Jabiru the guides are even reported to have complained that visiting tourists regularly know more about the Kakadu region and history than they do (Brady 1985:37). The problem is that the complexities of Aboriginal society take many months to learn. Ken Liberman, Western Desert Research Officer for the Western Australian Museum, notes:

> ...after two years of active [field work] contact I am only just beginning [myself] to understand the uniquely identifying objects of Aboriginality (Liberman 1978:158).

The problem which awakens such Euraustralian interpretation of the Dreamtime is that of trivialisation. "In popular European thinking, mythological beasts are equated with fairy tales, and the homilies they evoke are often associated with the need to educate and entertain children" (Lawrence 1985:101). Such reduced explanations, when applied to explanations of the Dreamtime, tend to inculcate little appreciation for the living continuous Aboriginal culture and are "more inclined to denigrate it" (ibid.). They imply no respect for the degree to which Aboriginal economics and ritual were interlocked, and too frequently the Aboriginal "longtime" [its dynamic belief system] is merely "treated as some kind of pantomime" (Dodson, 1984:35).

Proposition 2: Advance Motivation

Visitors' appreciation for Aboriginal sites and relics in Central and Northern Australia is likely to be influenced by the quality of pre-visit interpretation made available to them

In his landmark writings in the 1960s, Borstein expounded the view that travelers go to see only what they already know to be "there." The point was echoed in Australia by Derek Roff, Head Ranger at Uluru National Park in the 1970s:

> A lot of people [here at Ayers Rock, capturing the outback experience] don't know anything more about the park other than there's a big rock that turns red (Bosselman 1985).

Horne (1992:155, 367) considers that pre-interpretation (i.e. pre-visit "education") is critical for all heritage and cultural sites. Otherwise the tourism that people engage in remains merely as "involuntary as the functions of the autonomic nervous system." Thus, in Horne's terms, what travel marketeers and tourism planners must learn to cater for is enriching forms of "sight -experiencing" rather than perfunctory forms of "sightseeing" (ibid.:132–137, 382). If important cultural sites are to be promoted, travel marketeers and tourism planners have a responsibility to engender among tourists the *darshana* (the Hindu word for the mysterious ecstasy) of a place (ibid.:28, 377). To that end, Hollinshead (1996:336–8) suggests that the development of precious storylines about Aboriginal Australia should focus much more adroitly upon the mystical numenosity of the particular Aboriginal group/culture/inheritance rather than being maintained on object-based, phenomenologically dependent presentations. Such advance projection of numenosity is no simple task, however—and it is highly demanding of consultative prowess (ibid.:335–44).

Proposition 3: Market Segmentation

Visitors range considerably in the degree to which they seek genuine contact with a host Aboriginal community

As in most marketing exercises, the key to the successful promotion of Aboriginal sites in Central and Northern Australia principally lies with market segmentation, the reciprocal process by which the most appropriate mix of travelers is encouraged to visit respective sites and those sites are enhanced to suit the measured interests of those specific travelers. The techniques of such segmentation approaches are relatively new to outback Australia. Existing observational literature of tourist activity at Aboriginal sites is littered with references to the presence or behavior of unacceptable or "high risk" tourists. While Gale and Jacobs have advised on the main groups are that place Aboriginals' art in danger (Gale and Jacobs 1986:4), others have voiced condemnation of inadequate management surveillance systems at sites of immense ritual significance: for example, at King's Canyon in Central Australia, "visitors had been ... washing themselves and their clothes in the waterhole at Lilla Creek, [which is the vital and revered] part of the mythological tradition of the possum" (Hamilton 1984:373).

In many instances access conditions to Aboriginal sites have acted as a default segmenter, giving rise to the predominance of a high proportion of visitors who espouse the four-wheel-drive tradition (Brady 1985:15).

The Aboriginal people themselves, of course, automatically practice forms of visitor selection. When asked if there are any restrictions on people attending ceremonies or watching initiation ceremonies, an Aboriginal elder, Harry Diagamara replied: "It all depends. It comes back to attitudes. The [local Aboriginal] people will watch you when you get onto the reserve or settlement, and if you're really doing your best and you're fair dinkum, then you'll be invited" (Tatz 1975:80).

Given that the improved transport connections and facility levels of the eighties and nineties will considerably widen the range of interest and preferences of tourists visiting the outback, it is imperative that a comprehensive effort is taken to locate close-at-hand sites of low ritual significance that can be tapped for "rapid-transport/low contact" visitation, and it is critical elsewhere to determine the scale and scope of tourism possible at other more distant sites. At each respective site the form of accommodation, the range of educational tours, and the offered length of stay should all be selected with reference to the appropriate segment of visitors that the condition and preciousness of the available heritage can "service."

Proposition 4: Land and the Old-Time Way

Aboriginal self-esteem and group support for tourism ventures will be enhanced where the legal primacy of Aboriginal ownership of the place in question is asserted

The land has always been the heart of the Aboriginal people, an inseparable part of their being. They believe they came from the earth, they must tend it, and at death they will return to it. Land ownership is thus central to all understanding of their struggle to survive:

> The land itself was their chapel, and their shrines were hills and creeks and their religious relics were animals, plants, and birds. Thus the migrations of Aboriginals though spurred by economic need, were also pilgrimages (Blainey 1976:202).

Unfortunately, "There are no English words good enough to give a sense of the Aboriginal group and its homeland" (Japanangka and Nathan 1983:11). For them the land is patterned with the mythical tracks of *tjukurpa* (the Dreamtime) where their Forefathers established the ranges, the billabongs and the forests. Each site has a spiritual existence and is maintained today by approved custodians. Accordingly, "It is more correct to say that the land possesses the men than it is to say that the men possess the land" (Liberman 1978:162). Put another way, the Aboriginal people not only come from the land, they are the land. In Pitjantjatjara language in central Australia, this relationship of the tie of people to the land is conveyed by the single concept *ngura*, whilst the people themselves are called *anangu*, "the human beings who belong to the earth" (Toyne and Vachon 1984:5). Hence:

> *Ngangatja apu yiya, ngayuku tjamu*—This is not a rock, it is my grandfather (ibid.).

Consequently when an Aboriginal speaks of earth he frequently means, in a powerful and symbolic sense, his "shoulder" or his "side" (Japanangka and Nathan 1983:11).

The pain for the Pitjantjatjara and related peoples of central Australia is that

the twentieth century has seen them "drawn out of their *ngura* in the desert,"
and as Euraustralians forced change upon their social and religious structures
"the lives of *anangu* were being regimented and controlled by others" (Toyne
and Vachon 1984:34). Thus today the Aboriginal people of central Australia
and elsewhere wish to regain control of their lives. It is fundamentally a question of cultural identity. Anangu wish to live off the land, their land, without
degrading it:

> I think of the land as the history of my nation. It tells me how we came into being,
> and what system we must live (Galarrwuy Yunupingu) [N. Territory Tourist Com-
> mission n.d.:4).

While Euraustralians are inclined to have a "distaste for anything which is not
under control" (Liberman 1978:167), Aboriginals tend to have an object-free
society, and by extension do not wish to reify and control nature as Euraustralians
do, as if it were a material possession. Aboriginal people seek to relate to an
untouched land, an entity irrespective of state borders... "one land, one law, one
people" (Toyne and Vachon 1984:39).

Thus the Aboriginal Land Rights (N.T.) Act in 1976 was a document long-
awaited by Aboriginal groups. It has pioneered "homeland" legislation in Australia, providing a legal framework for Aboriginal groups to make claim upon
unalienated Crown-land with respect to "traditional attachment." Seven years
later (11 December 1983), Prime Minister Hawke announced the intent to transfer
the title of Ayers Rock in central Australia back to Aboriginal people as inalien-
able freehold, and now the majestic and vital site is leased back in the Australian National Park and Wildlife Service where the Aboriginal people have a
majority on the Board of Management. But not all governments in Australia are
so enlightened, and the N.T. Tourist Commission has made its own more aggressive stance about the threat of the loss of Ayers Rock and such lead sites
very clear. At Kakadu National Park, for instance, a submission to the Alligator
River State II land claim in November 1980 included the following expressed
aim:

> To undertake controlled development of tourism resources and achieve the sig-
> nificant economic growth for the N.T. Community *unrestricted access must be
> provided* to international and domestic travelers to Kakadu National Parks, *with-
> out let or hindrance, no, or in the future, by private or ethnic ownership* (Brady
> 1985:17 [her emphasis]).

The message that must be conveyed to tourists and to new tourist operators is
that the whole land was and is still "religious." It is not a mere question of
fencing off small distinct "sacred places." The land and the law are one, indivis-
ible. "The Aboriginal people are sustained only by their own strength and integrity, and by their spiritual attachment to the land" (Japanangka and Nathan
1983:6). Thus, whilst Aboriginal people increasingly accept that their land is of
interest to people from all over Australia and overseas, and are increasingly

content for visitation to occur, they wish to have freehold title and *the major say* on development. The Pitjantjatjara Council proposal for Uluru included the following statement:

> The Whiteman has known of these places only a little time and he cannot own them, and they are not his country.... We must protect our law, our sacred places from visitors. These are for Aboriginals alone and essential to us if our culture is to survive (Layton 1986:107).

Proposition 5: Exploitation or Management-in-Sympathy?

Aboriginal groups will support tourism ventures which provide them with the opportunity to maintain control of space and the speed of development

European law and institutions have been slow to recognize the capability of Aboriginal people to direct the course of their own collective lives. Though the much praised Aboriginal Land Rights (Northern Territory) Act of 1976 was a considerable step forward, subsequent land claim hearings have continued to relegate Aboriginal people to a "Fourth World" status as a minority group which must lease land back to the Australian National Parks and Wildlife Service even though traditional ownership is acknowledged (George Chaloupka in Sullivan 1984:65). The first plan of management for Kakadu National Park provides a good case in point. While the plan clearly identified the need to protect the landscape as a living tradition of Aboriginal society, it made no provision for an Aboriginal board of management, and was only concerned with "narrow aspects of Aboriginal culture" (ibid.:68). Historically, too many experiments with Aboriginal people have failed because they have continued to place Aborigines "in situations where they felt themselves looked down upon by the whites" (Reynolds 1981:153). Euraustralian institutions continue to project an air of patronage over Aboriginals. Collectively, Euraustralians fail to recognize that whatever is an Aborigine's appearance (in relation to Western perspectives on dress and presentation!) he or she does have his/her own dignity and his/her own sought freedom. As a corollary, Aborigines are themselves easily frustrated by the inequalities of white society. They remain "the most administered section of the Australian population," facing enormous federal, state and community resources and bureaucratic structures which appear to provide "more benefit to administrators and staff than to Aboriginal people themselves" (Toyne and Vachon 1984:154).

Aboriginal groups in Australia largely wish to have "control" in the decision-making apparatus of park and tourist sites on their land. This does not mean they want administrative or executive power over management. They mainly crave a strong voice in negotiation and regular consultation, as the Maori of New Zealand crave *rangatiratanga* (the ability of their various peoples to have authority and control over their own affairs and resources) (Hall

1996:168). The key aspect for most aboriginal groups/communities in Australia is *who has the right to speak for a particular sacred site or piece of
land*—i.e., which individual has the inherited right to comment upon it, about
it, and for it. Thus the Aboriginal management presence for a given "tourism"
site should be viewed as *a collection of personalities* who possess the inherited
right to make judgments when the occasion demands rather than as a full-time
or rigid administrative body. As for the Maori (Hall 1996:172–3), only those
who "own" the given site can speak for a site. "Administration" and even "residence" are therefore divorced from "ownership," and Aboriginals, accordingly,
do not need to make clear-cut distinctions in terms of ethnicity or color on
those two matters (Lawrence 1984:54). The situation was neatly surmised by
Ginger Packsaddle when speaking about the Amandibji land he and his people
have recently re-inherited southwest of Katherine:

> When [the famous pioneer] Durack came into this country, he need blackfella to
> help him. But things are different now, and we need white fella to help us, white
> fella more savvy, know everything about moneyside, about cheque book. My
> people build yards, they fence, they do stockwork but Amanbidji need black and
> white to work together ("The Miracle..." 1987).

Proposition 6: Choice of Contact Circumstance

*Aboriginal groups view encounters with tourists from "best", which they
dictate themselves, to "worst", which are initiated by tourists or the tourism
industry*

What the Aborigines appear to want above all is for governments "to trust the
Aboriginal peoples' capacity to manage their own affairs" (H.C. Coombs in
Japanangka and Nathan 1983:vii–viii). This, in terms of tourism does not necessarily mean a rejection of the encroachment of the industry, it means that
where the tourist product is located, it must be done "to ensure that Aborigines
have enough room to avoid the tourist encounter when they choose to do so"
(Palmer 1985, 131; [my emphasis]). It is a rejection of exploitation and abuse—
a question of squashed pride. Aboriginal people in park and tourist areas need
their space and sanctity (Ross 1991)—a vital and sustaining community re-
quirement which De Burlo (1996:226) has found to be particularly important
elsewhere for peoples in the South Pacific, specifically for the Sa of Vanuatu.

Proposition 7: Living History

*Aboriginal groups will support tourism ventures which help the community
relocate to their homeland(s) where they can live with restored pride,
independence and dignity*

In the two hundred years since the founding of Sydney (1788) and white settlement in Australia, "The mark of successful settlements has been the transfor-

mation of national landscapes into simulacra of Europe" (Hamilton 1984:365). This orientation has also applied to tourism, where the Euraustralian concept of spirituality is abstract, and tends to be shaped around a commodified perspective on the definition of heritage (Hollinshead 1993a,b; 1996:328–44). In this sense "it can take the form of a separation of sites from their land" and it has an emphasis on listing and collecting objects and bounded sites" (Rowse and Moran 1985:81).

A sorry consequence of this "incomplete" or "unsatisfactory" orientation was uncovered by Warwick Dix, former Registrar of Aboriginal sites for the Western Australia Museum. In studying the state's 1972 Aboriginal Heritage Act, he concluded that it merely afforded protection to *"places,"* not to the *continuous living inheritance*, and moreover to "small clearly defined places at that" (Dix 1978:81). Thus the predominant Euraustralian view of the Aboriginal heritage has been a static and hyper-selective one, where only supreme sites are catalogued and preserved. To all intents and purposes this is a manifestation of the Yellowstone *ecosphere* model of the National Park idea (Stevens 1986:4). Emphasis is thereby placed restrictively on the protection of unique national features, with a guaranteed right of public access. More appropriate for Aboriginal interests, however, might be some form of translation of the British National Park concept (ibid.: 16). The key emphasis in Britain is upon received and appreciated heritage, not upon wilderness per se. Under British *biosphere* thinking, the protected landscape is singled out not just for its beauty or national-historic value alone, but for the fashion in which it is today "entwined with people as part of the landscape" (ibid.: 17). The preservation protects a landscape which is felt to have contemporary "living" cultural value, not just a historical significance. The parallels between the Englishness of distant Britain and Aboriginal Australia are surprisingly close, perhaps:

> Landscape features, particularly those which lie near our homes form part of our collective identity. We are, in part, the places that have shaped our lives. If England's landscape is impoverished, so are our personalities (Shoard 1981:106).

Accordingly, indigenous people must play a key role in all levels of planning regarding large tracts of country and within National Parks. "Every effort should be made to achieve the desired conservation objective with minimum disruption of traditional ways of life and maximum benefit to local people" (ibid.:670).

Proposition 8: Cognition of Tourism

Tourism ventures to Aboriginal settlements are likely to be more popularly received by Aborigines if they provide the potential for the host community to establish personal contact with visitors

The manner in which individual Aboriginal communities will respond to the opportunities and challenge of tourism will depend largely upon their attitude toward the industry. Clearly one of the problems to be faced is that of cognitive dissonance on the part of some Aboriginals brought about by their complete lack of exposure to the phenomenon of tourism (Ross 1991). The problem is currently being encountered in the Purnululu [Bungle Bungle] National Park in Western Australia where the Warmun Community of Turkey Creek has been found to have a limited knowledge of tourism and tourist operations and a narrow understanding of the occidental concept of parks (Foster 1986:20). The problem is similar to that of contemporary Australian law, where parallels may be drawn to the inability of Aboriginals to understand courtroom procedure (Liberman 1978:174). Lawrence has, however, written lucidly on the matter for the Kakadu region. He concludes that ideas on "tourism" and "tourists" are not uniform in Aboriginal thought, principally on account of the crucial distinction Aborigines make between individuals and groups. Accordingly:

> *Tourism* is thought of as 'a lot of people' and as such is not to be valued; 'we don't want tourism' was a common refrain. But *tourists* can be different, as they have the potential *to be identified as individuals* (Lawrence 1985:62 [my emphasis]).

Having been initially bewildered by Aborigines' "disquieting tendency ... to speak either positively or negatively of tourism and then within minutes entirely reverse their opinion" (ibid.), Lawrence concludes that Aborigines he interviewed were not vacillating, or trying to be 'agreeable' but were rather making a distinction between the institution and its parts, thus:

> The concept of *tourism* invokes the notion of an invasion and is therefore not compatible with traditional ideas of how to protect the land. But individuals, whether explorers, hunters, or *tourists*, have always been more or less welcome because they can be dealt with singly (ibid. [my emphasis]).

The pivotal factor is whether a relationship/encounter with a tourist has *the potential to be "personal."* If a one-to-one relationship can be created with a specific visitor(s), Lawrence concludes that Aboriginal people will "go out of their way to ensure that their guests are well taken care of" (ibid.:64). If it cannot, Aborigines will be inclined to retreat to the generic attitude toward tourism in general.

But Lawrence adds a second important point. Aboriginal people do not regard tourists with a undimensional reality, but "rather they possess distinctive personae based on the places they frequent and the activities they pursue" (ibid.:65). Indeed Aborigines do not always know who, per se, the tourists are, vis-à-vis government personnel, mine employees and other locals. The difficulty from the Aboriginal perspective is that tourists just do not stay around long enough:

> They do not, usually, get beyond the first stages of the measuring up process. They enter Kakadu as an amorphous entity, engage in activities that identify [to Aborigines] their particular purpose and then leave. [The Aborigines] scarcely have the opportunity to make them part of their own world. If foreigners are to be

accepted as a group [paradoxically] they must first present their credentials individually. Tourists do this in their own peculiar and hurried fashion, but they seldom stay around long enough to gather up their diploma. The Aborigines can understand and appreciate the camping and fishing, but they cannot quite grasp why it ends or why the candidates leave (ibid.:68).

The Aboriginal world-order does not permit "strangers." There can be no outsiders in Aboriginal cosmology. Everyone has to be "placed" in relation to the host community, or more precisely, to the spiritualities of the "Dreamtime."

Proposition 9: Aboriginal Temporality

Tourist agencies wishing to develop dual or joint management arrangements with Aboriginal groups will be more likely to succeed if they can design co-operative mechanisms that respect the preferred consensual and spontaneous character of Aboriginal decision-making and preference for spontaneous activity

Aboriginal society is largely a society in stasis. In contrast to the Euraustralian world it is a non-progressive inherently conservative one, organized to further the blessings of *tjukurpa*, the creation period, longtime ago. Liberman has highlighted three main factors which inevitably contribute to this stable persistent world-order, though causal relationships have not been proven.

Firstly, adversarial debate is almost unknown in Aboriginal society, a reluctance in political direction which may result from "the extreme consequences [for individual] of any conflict" (Liberman 1978:159). Consequently, individual leadership has no revered legitimacy in Aboriginal society, and "each [person] is kept restrained by the others [in an] egalitarian mutuality" (ibid.). Secondly, society is non-egoistic whereby "innovations, formulations and decisions are dis-individualized [and] conclusions are arrived at without an egoistic concern for the persons involved" (ibid.:161). It is thus difficult for Aborigines to devote or dedicate themselves long-term to singular personal projects. Thirdly, Aborigines live as if "each time is sufficient unto itself ... and abandon themselves easily to the current enterprise they are taken up with" (ibid.:63). Thus, they are inclined to become involved with emergent spontaneous phenomenon almost in a re-active sense, and tend to lack the pro-active and time-specific concern for order and consistency of Euraustralians. These three factors combine to deny the cultivation of capitalist drive and constrain the development of free enterprise activity within the society. Overall therefore, Aborigines lack the ambitious self image of Euraustralians, a characteristic which undoubtedly prevents the competitive or elevated displays of worth. In lieu of a strong drive-of-initiative, Aboriginal actions tend to be typified by acquiescent stances, a retreatist approach which is hardly the kind of ambition to empower commercial operations in tourism (Altman and Finlayson 1991).

Proposition 10: Work Routines

Aboriginal people favor those forms of work experience in tourism which permit them to cement existing social relationships and to share in a kinship experience

Aborigines do not generally possess the Euraustralian sense of morality towards work, and this can become something which inevitably causes problems when communities engage in tourism. When three Aboriginal rangers were appointed at Ayers Rock in central Australia in the mid-1970s, difficulties resulted on account of the un-Aboriginal work patterns ... an occurrence also voiced by Bill Neiijie, an Aboriginal employee of the Australian National Parks and Wildlife service at Kakadu (Sullivan 1984:42). The Ayers Rock rangers also found their job troublesome because they found the role of cross-cultural guide hard to embrace. Aborigines are unable and unwilling to modernize "overnight" as, for instance, some indigenous groups in New Guinea have been able to do in almost a single season (Liberman 1978:169). Aborigines feel especially uncomfortable in ephemeral relations (Brady 1985:23). At the same time some members of the community did not approve of the fact that single individuals should ever be earning wages from explaining the stories of Uluru (Layton 1986:96).

There are many barriers which prevent Aborigines from fully committing themselves to the regular and consistent work routines that the tourism industry demands (Lawlor 1991). Most Aborigines have little or no formal education, and reading and writing skills are essential if park or tourism service management techniques are to be followed. Retention rates on training programs are not high (Lawrence 1985:196), while the sheer shyness of many Aboriginal people proves to be another constraint (Bill Neiijie in Sullivan 1984:42). Work in traditional Aboriginal society is a form of functional co-operative effort performed via the kinship system. The incumbent and accountable task of tourism operators and entrepreneurs who wish to work with Aborigines is to find a modern method or *modus vivendi* of inducing that co-operative endeavor. A new ritual and respect for work is demanded. In indigenous locales, ourism cannot develop at a rate faster than the support community institutions can allow.

Implications

The propositions offered in this chapter have implications for public and private sector practitioners working in tourism with and alongside Aborigines, as well as for industry researchers. A number of the more critical implications are now presented below in the form of suggested guidelines for those who are responsible for marketing decisions with respect to the establishment or development of Aboriginal tourism schemes.

It is imperative that agencies become fully acquainted with *the particulari-ties of the Aboriginal group* in question. Not all Aboriginal groups are versed with, for example, the didgeridoo or boomerang. When Captain Philip Sydney came to find the first colonial settlement in 1788, the continent was divided by "hundreds of fluid republics [divided] by barriers of language, geography, my-thology, or blood" (Blainey 1983:31). Though the scale may be different today, these disparities still exist. It is unwise to regard Aboriginal people as one simi-lar community, therefore (Lawlor 1991). Co-operative decisions must be seeded at the local level and not first bureaucratized in, for instance, Canberra. There is minimum place or potential for the flown-in, short-term, instant expert or consultant.

Practitioners should respect the right of Aboriginal people *not to reveal* their religious and ceremonial sites (Cowan 1989). Just as mining companies do not need to know the location, size or significance of sacred sites (they merely need to know where they can operate with confidence) (Toyne and Vachon 1984:114), so tourism agencies need only know the extent and whereabouts of those foci the responsible indigenous owners deem it safe and propitious to proclaim.

Practitioners should learn not to expect *consistent advice* from Aboriginal advisers (Lawlor 1991). Aboriginal opinions and political influences in any given area are very much a matter of personalities and local sway (Palmer 1985:130). On the other hand, one should beware the false Aboriginal consen-sus. Aborigines generally have no wish to be offensive and "their chief tactic is to agree with whatever 'the whitefella' wants but to be committed to nothing" (Liberman 1978:169).

Practitioners need to build *flexibility* into the *site decision* and *operational arrangements* for any concentrated resort development on or near an Aborigi-nal settlement so that the Aborigines have enough room to *avoid the tourist encounter* whenever they need or wish to do so. Whenever possible, built struc-tures should be retained within those areas already made available to tourists, and considerable thought must be given to methods of enforcing designated access arrangements. It is crucial that Aborigines are encouraged to remain traditionally Aboriginal in thought and experience yet free to exploit the advan-tages of contemporary Euraustralian contact at their own will (Cowan 1991).

Practitioners planning to employ Aboriginal people must build flexibility into their operations to take account of the Aboriginal rhythm of life in view of the poor retention rates on existing training programs (Lawlor 1991). In this respect, the Australian National Park and Wildlife service has already intro-duced less regimented "public service" conditions such as new leave-without-pay formulas (Hill 1985:62). Further imaginative thought needs to be applied to every facet of Aboriginal training and employment, so that individuals from the host community can fulfill both their inherited cultural and social obliga-tions as well as their cross-cultural 'whitefella' demands.

Inter-disciplinary perspectives must be brought to the examination of development issues in tourism. The anthropologist, the behavioral scientists, and the market researcher have clearly not gathered together sufficiently. While this chapter is largely an appeal for marketeers to spend time and effort getting to appreciate the Aboriginal world-order, it is just as important for those already conversant with Aboriginal values to cultivate an objective and fuller awareness of tourism as a field and for marketing as its instrument. In characterizing cultural tourism at Aboriginal sites in Queensland for archeologists, for example, K.A. Sutcliffe dismisses tourism as being "simply descriptive of going to look and to learn something of the resources that we possess as the visible links with the past" (Sutcliffe 1980:96). The motivations for and identifications within tourism are clearly much more diverse than this, Sutcliffe appears to suggest. Similarly, the statement "for the average tourist, the site and surrounding environment must appeal visually..." (ibid.:98) rides roughshod over the sensitivities of market analysis. There is no such animal as an average tourist! Such blanket observations do justice to neither the attributes of the previous site nor to the psychographic profile of the inquiring traveler. Indeed one of the reasons for the success of the planning process at Uluru in Central Australia appears to have been the bridging role played by the park management liaison officer, Ross Johnston. He had previously extensive experience with both the Mitijulu community and the promotional agency, the Australian National Parks and Wildlife Service (Foster 1986:12). Such a combination of interest and knowledge is most rare, however, it normally and critically must be force-fed across agencies.

Wherever possible, tourism and travel activities at or nearby Aboriginal communities should be developed at a relatively moderate rate to reduce the disintegrative and deleterious socio-cultural, economic, geo-physical and spiritual intrusions—something with which Sofield (1996:183) has, for instance, long advocated for tourism development in the indigenous Solomons. The Northern Territory, in particular, currently exhibits an expansionist aura in terms of government and entrepreneurial activity in Australia.

A Northern Territory Development Council spokesman said the Territory tourist industry was set to explode as the tourism jigsaw puzzle of attractions, marketing, transport and accommodation finally slotted into place (*N.T. News* 1984). The Northern Territory atmosphere here smacks of aggressive at-all-costs development, and of coercive acculturation through tourism. Even anthropologists in central Australia have occasionally thoughtlessly abused their privilege of power over Aboriginal people, such as with C.P. Mountford's publication of taboo photographs in his "Nomads of the Central Desert" text (Toyne and Vachon 1984:51). The pervasive attitude must be one of respect for Aboriginal institutions. This is especially crucial when material advantage is concerned. There may be merit, for instance, in encouraging Aboriginal people to "sacrifice" one site for tourist visitation in order that others can remain obscure and safe from impact. Problems can result, however, from the distinct patrician ownership of such sites. The selection of one site for "development" while others are excluded can bring about an imbalance of "profit" for some and "material disadvantage" for others (Sullivan 1984:30). The marketing agency needs to be adroitly and eclectically constructed to handle the geocultural circumspection that should accompany what at first might appear to be such seemingly straightforward development decisions.

Practitioners must properly *position infrastructure* to achieve properly paced change:

> Non-Aboriginal Australians may be able to cope with a freeway running past a cathedral, but Aboriginal people may consider a site forever desecrated if an open cut mine or major road is located nearby (Toyne and Vachon 1984:113).

Such desecration does not just apply to the land, it also applies to the people themselves, particularly if the built facility contains an outlet for alcohol. Traditionally, Aborigines had no knowledge of alcohol fermentation (Blainey 1976:173), and did not readily know how to control its effects within the social community. The difficulty today is that whenever Europeans administer the availability of alcohol they are usually tempted "to relinquish their responsibility" on the matter (Lawrence 1985:121). Success in the enforcement of access to alcohol tends to occur where the decisions are left to stable Aboriginal organizations (Palmer 1985:134). Given the pre-eminent place of alcohol in social settings for many sectors of the tourist market, it is thereby imperative that the placement of tourist amenities are therefore fully and widely aired with Aboriginal interest groups from the outset. They must be permitted leverage to dictate their own preferred enforcement regime. Euraustralian vigilance may just not be sufficiently consistent, or otherwise free from the taint of patronage, to succeed alone.

Practitioners must recognize that Aboriginal people are not the mere "passive victims of technological change ... but are seizing its advantages to continually re-establish their spiritual and social connections" (Toyne and Vachon 1984:19). Contrary to popular opinion, the evidence indicates that Aborigines have always been "curious about white society" and have endeavored to incorporate new experiences into their own world-order, provided they actually fitted "within the resilient bonds of traditional culture" (Reynolds 1981:2). The task for the tourism industry is to find attractive and relevant ways in which traditional owners can become involved in tourist enterprises focused on their traditional and contemporary stories, whether it be in terms of:

- equity
- direct employment
- construction
- concessionary arrangements
- interpretation, and/or
- maintenance (Foster 1986:21).

And, finally, if a satisfactory management capability for the inherited or emergent Aboriginal interests cannot be identified, that government agency should muster the courage to refuse the given "external" development for the interim. This final recommendation is one of *perpetuity*, and applies particularly to government instrumentalities charged with a responsibility for caring for and developing Aboriginal sites. On occasions, the appeal of Aboriginal lore and the attraction of the country will prove overwhelming and ripe for "promotion." But tourism is a force that can destroy uncomprehendingly and unintentionally the very treasure it seeks to reveal. In this respect the 1985 House of Representatives Standing Committee on Environment and Conservation in Australia merits praise for its measured decision to resist the opening up of the newly prominent Bungle Bungle massif in Western Australia (House of Representatives 1985:26). Questions of lasting heritage must take precedence over the demands for immediate industry benefit, if sustained mutual gain is to result.

Such are some of the complex ethnocentric and interpretive issues involved in the fascinating frenzy to market indigenous ritual, reality, and revelation downunder.

References

Altman, J.C. (1989) "Tourism Dilemmas for Aboriginal Australia." *Annals of Tourism Research* 16:456–76.

Altman, J.C. and J. Finlayson (1991) *Aborigines and Tourism*. An issues paper prepared for the Ecological Sustainable Working Group on Tourism. Canberra: Center for Aboriginal Economic Policy Research, Australian National University.

Blainey, G. (1976) *The Triumph of the Nomads*. Melbourne: Sun Books.

Bosselman, F.P. (1985) "The Promotion of Tourism and its Effect on Aborigines." In *Aborigines and Tourism: A Study of the Impact of Tourism on Aborigines in the Kakadu Region* (edited by Palmer, K.). Darwin NT: Northern Land Council.

Brady, M. (1985) "The Promotion of Tourism and its Effects on Aborigines." In *Aborigines and Tourism: A Study of the Impact of Tourism on Aborigines in the Kakadu Region* (edited by Palmer, K.). Darwin NT: Northern Land Council.

Burton-Taylor, J. (1996) "Cultural Rejuvenation." *Australian Way: Quantas In-Flight Magazine*, July, 76–80.

Butler, R. and T. Hinch, eds. (1996). *Tourism and Indigenous Peoples*. London: International Thomson Business Press.

Cater, E. (1987) "Tourism in the Least Developed Countries." *Annals of Tourism Research* 14:220.

Cowan, J. (1989) *Mysteries of the Dreamtime: The Spiritual Life of Australian Aboriginies*. Bridgeport, Dorset: Prism Press.

De Burlo, C. (1996) "Cultural Resistance and Ethnic Tradition on South Pentecost, Vanatu." In *Tourism and Indigenous Peoples* (edited by Butler, R. and Hinch, T.), 255–76. London: International Thomson Business Press.

Department of the Chief Minister of the Northern Territory (1984) *Aboriginals and the Tourists' View: A Guide for Tour Operators in the N. Territory, Darwin.*

Dix, W. (1978) "The Aboriginal Heritage Act of 1972." In *"Whitefella Business"— Aborigines in Australian Politics* (edited by Howard, M.C.), 81–2. Philadelphia: Institute for the Study of Human Issues.

Dodson, P. (1984) *Aboriginal Culture.* Department of the Chief Minister of the Northern Territory, 332-8.

Ellis, R. (1984) *Tourism and the Aboriginal Culture: Some Observations.* Department of the Chief Minister of the Northern Territory.

Foster, D. (1986) *Planning Issues Arising in Purnululu (Bungle Bungle) National Park: A Report to the Warmun Community of Turkey Creek, Bundoora, Victoria.* Phillip Institute of Technology, Department of Leisure Studies.

Gale, F. and J. Jacobs (1986) "Identifying High-Risk Visitors at Aboriginal Art Sites in Australia." *Rock Art Research* 3(1):3–19.

Gray, F. du P. (1973) "On Safari." *New York Review of Books,* 28 June, 25–9.

Hall, C.M. (1994) *"Tourism and Politics: Policy, Power and Place.* London: Belhaven.

Hall, C.M. (1996) "Tourism and the Maori of Aotearoa, New Zealand." In *Tourism and Indigenous Peoples* (edited by Butler, R. and Hinch, T.). London: International Thomson Business Press.

Hamilton, A. (1984) *Spoon-feeding the Lizards: Culture and Conflict in Central Australia.* Meanjin 3:369–78.

Hill, M. (1985) "Kakadu National Park: An Australian Approach to Joint Management." *Environment* 17(3):57–64.

Hollinshead, K. (1993a) "Encounters in Tourism." In *VNR Encyclopedia of Hospitality and Tourism* (edited by Kahn, M.A., Olson, M.D. and Var, T.), 636–51. New York: Van Nostrand Reinhold.

Hollinshead, K. (1993b) "Ethnocentrism in Tourism." In *VNR Encyclopedia of Hospitality and Tourism* (edited by Kahn, M.A., Olson, M.D. and Var, T.), 652–61. New York: Van Nostrand Reinhold.

Hollinshead, K. (1996) "Marketing and Metaphysical Realism: The Disidentification of Aboriginal Life and Traditions Through Tourism." In *Tourism and Indigenous Peoples* (edited by Butler, R. and Hinch, T.), 308–49. London: International Thomson Business Press.

Hollinshead, K. and C. De Burlo (In Press) *Journeys into Otherness: The Representation of Difference and Identity in Cultural and Public Tourism.* London: Routledge.

Horne, D. (1992) *The Intelligent Tourist.* McMahon's Point, NSW: Margaret Gee Publishing.

House of Representatives: Standing Committee on Environment and Conservation (1985) *Protection of the Bungle Bungle.* Canberra: Australian Government Publishing Service.

Japanangka, D.L. and P. Nathan (1983) *Settle Down Country: A Community Report for the Central Australian Aboriginal Congress.* Malmsbury, Victoria: Kibble Books and Central Australian Congress.

Lawrence, R. (1985) "The Tourist Impact and the Aboriginal Response." In *Aborigines and Tourism: A Study of the Impact of Tourism on Aborigines in the Kakadu Region, Northern Territory* (edited by Palmer, K.). Darwin: Northern Land Council.

Lawlor, R. (1991) *Voices of the First Day: Awakening in the Aboriginal Dreamtime.* Rochester, VT: Inner Traditions.

Layton, R. (1991) *Uluru: An Aboriginal History of Ayers Rock.* Canberra: Australian Institute of Aboriginal Studies.

Liberman, K. (1978) "Ontology and Cultural Politics: Aboriginal Versus European Australians." *Dialect and Anthropology* 3(2):157–76.

Lundberg, D.E. (1985) "Tourism as a Force of Imperialism." In *Hosts and Guests: The Anthropology of Tourism* (edited by Smith, V.L.). Philadelphia: University of Pennsylvania Press.

"The Miracle of Amanbidji" (1987) *Weekend Australian*, 27–28 June.

Nash, D. (1977) "Tourism as a Force of Imperialism." In *Hosts and Guests: The Anthropology of Tourism* (edited by Smith, V.L.). Philadelphia: University of Pennsylvania Press.

Northern Territory Tourist Commision (n.d.) *People of Two Times.* Darwin.

N.T. News (1984) 25 October, 3.

Palmer, K., ed. (1985) *Aborigines and Tourism: A Study of the Impact of Tourism on Aborigines in the Kakadu Region, Northern Territory.* Darwin: Northern Land Council.

Reynolds, H. (1981) *The Other Side of the Frontier: Aboriginal Resistance to the European Invasion of Australia.* Ringwood: Penguin.

Roff, D. (1984) "Visitor Behaviour and Management." In *Visitors to Aboriginal Sites: Access, Control and Management.* Proceedings of the 1983 Kakadu Workshop (edited by Sullivan, H.), 54–6. Canberra: Australian National Wildlife Services.

Ross, H. (1991) "Controlling Access to Environment and Self: Aboriginal Perspectives on Tourism." *Australian Psychologist* 26(3):176–82.

Rowse, T. and A. Moran (1985) "Particularly Australian—The Poltiical Construction of Cultural Identity." *Australian Society*, 229–77.

Selwyn, T. (1996) *The Tourism Image: Myths and Myth Making in Tourism.* Chichester: John Wiley and Sons.

Shoard, M. (1981) "Why Landscapes Are Harder to Protect than Buildings." In *Our Past Before Us: Why Do We Save It?* (edited by Lowenthal, D. and Binney, M.), 83–108. London: Temple Smith.

Smith, V.L., ed. (1977). *Hosts and Guests: The Anthropology of Tourism.* Philadelphia: University of Pennsylvania Press.

Sofield, T.H.B. (1996) In *Tourism and Indigenous Peoples* (edited by Butler, R. and Hinch, T.), 176–202. London: International Thomson Business Press.

Stevens, S. (1986) "Inhabited National Parks: Indigenous Peoples in Protected Landscapes." In *East Kimberley Working Paper No. 10.* Canberra: Australian National Prks and Wildlife Service.

Sullivan, S. (1986) *Visitors to Aboriginal Sites: Access, Control and Management.* Proceedings of the 1983 Kakadu Workshop. Canberra: Australian National Wildlife Services.

Sutcliffe, G. (1984) *Cultural Tourism in Queensland.* Aracheology Paper 15. Fortitude Valley, Queensland: Deparment of Aboriginal and Islander Advancement.

Swain, M.B. (1977) "Cuna Women and Ethnic Tourism: A Way to Persist and an Avenue to Change." In *Hosts and Guests: The Anthropology of Tourism* (edited by Smith, V.L.), 71–81. Philadelphia: University of Pennsylvania Press.

Tatz, C., ed. (1975) *Black Viewpoints: The Aboriginal Experience.* Sydney: Australia and New Zealand Book Company.

Toyne, P. and D. Vachon (1984) *Growing Up the Country: The Pitjantjatjara Struggle for Their Land.* Ringwood: Penguin.

Turner, L. and Ash, J. (1975) *The Golden Hordes: International Tourism and the Pleasure Periphery.* London: Constable.

3

THE HERITAGE EMBROGLIO: QUAGMIRES OF POLITICS, ECONOMICS, AND "TRADITION"

CLODAGH BRENNAN HARVEY

Even as recently as ten years ago the traveler to Ireland, or any intrepid soul with a mission there, might easily find himself or herself on a solitary journey in the countryside, braving unpredictable weather conditions, challenging unyielding terrain, or charting an untrodden path in the pursuit, following perhaps the meandering directions provided by some helpful, loquacious native. Indeed, the pristine beauty of Ireland's countryside, the quietude, the sense of space and privacy that it affords, the friendliness of its inhabitants, and the antiquity of its traditions and way of life, have long been among the most salient aspects of Ireland's appeal and of its promotion in tourist literature, both at home and abroad.[1] Tourism has played a central role in Ireland's economy and in its cultural life for well over a century (O'Connor 1993b:69) and promises to have an even greater impact in the future; the steady, continuing development of international tourism indicates that it may well become the world's largest single source of employment by the end of this decade (O'Connor 1993a:1).

One result of this economic trend is the remarkable number of representations of Ireland's material and nonmaterial culture which have emerged in the last decade in both urban and rural settings, and ever more frequently (although not invariably) in response to the demands—and the financial inducements—of the tourist industry. Heritage and interpretive centers, museums and theme parks, summer schools and festivals of almost every description, and extremely sophisticated, pyrotechnical amusements depicting aspects of Irish history and "tradition" now confront visitor and native alike at almost every turn.[2] This sudden outcropping of heritage attractions has met with almost universal opposition from museum professionals, historians, archaeologists, literary scholars, and other cultural specialists. Most frequently, such opposition is based upon the putative inauthenticity of many heritage attractions and upon the trivialization, over-simplification, or commodification of culture or history that they may represent. While these concerns are certainly legitimate, they represent merely the tip of the heritage iceberg: under the surface the enticements of heritage funding have often set individuals, institutions, and political bodies scrambling with each other over limited goods, frequently rushing to implement potentially ill-conceived, short-sighted projects with no guarantee of on-going benefit to communities that may all too willingly embrace them. The overarching philosophical and historiographical issues remain the most complex: how accurately does any given representation reflect Irish history or culture and the Irish past, particularly the knotty and highly contested history of Northern Ireland? What images or stories should emerge to portray accurately Ireland's regional diversity, pluralistic histories, or the rapidly changing nature of contemporary Irish society? And just who should be charged with these all-important tasks? In this essay we will take a brief excursion through some important heritage attractions in the two Irelands, north and south, examining in the process some of the most salient cultural, economic, or political issues (or any combination of these) associated with each.

Museums, Heritage, and Interpretive Centers: The Funding Vortex

At the level of popular discourse, issues of authenticity, relevance, and ecological or economic viability are at the core of the heritage debate, as I have suggested. Much of the heat which has been generated by heritage projects here in Northern Ireland, however, and in Ireland generally, has been directly related to issues of funding, a situation which has to some degree pitted the proponents of heritage centers and museum (and gallery) professionals against each other, and which requires some explication.

The three major museums in Northern Ireland are established and maintained solely with funds from the Department of Education for Northern Ireland (DENI).[3] Heritage and interpretive centers, as part of a larger "leisure" segment, are eligible for the European Community (EC) Structural Funds and monies granted by the Northern Irish Tourist Board and the International Fund for Ireland which target development of the tourism sector, an increasingly important aspect of Northern Ireland's economy.[4] In both Northern Ireland and the Republic, the guidelines for investment in heritage attractions of various kinds have been carefully worked out while similar guidelines for investment in the museum sector remain conspicuously absent (Walsh 1993:43). The sums allocated for development of the leisure/tourism market, including the design and construction of heritage attractions, have been substantial and very enticing, and have frequently proved divisive.

Some recent examples are highly illustrative: the two-year period 1993–1994 saw an investment of £8.6 million ventured on visitor attractions designed to lure tourists to the city of Armagh (Co. Armagh) and its environs. These include the interpretive center Navan at Armagh (which alone represents an investment of over £4 million), the Palace Stables Heritage Centre, St Patrick's Trian (in which "The Land of Lilliput" is also housed), and the Eartharium and Astron Park at the Armagh Planetarium (*Belfast Telegraph* 6 January 1994; "Saints"). The new "Knight Ride" in Carrickfergus, which opened in 1993 and is currently the "highest tech" attraction in Northern Ireland, represents an investment of £3 million ("Saints"). A new visitor center interpreting the life of St Patrick and the complex of legends surrounding the saint has been proposed for Downpatrick (Co. Down), involving an initial capital outlay of £5 million (*Down Democrat* 27 October 1993). This plan has proved highly controversial, for not only is the proposed site for the new center an important and environmentally sensitive landmark in its own right, but it is also within eyeshot of the long-established Down County Museum which already boasts a small "Saint Patrick's Heritage Centre", thereby posing a threat to the museum's continued financial support (*Local History Link* 11 April 1994). The first level of the problem has thus been the differential access on the part of museums and heritage/interpretive centers to the generous funding earmarked for tourism.

A 1993 "Spotlight" documentary segment, "Saints, Scholars, and Heritage Centres," brought these and other submerged aspects of the heritage controversy to the surface by providing scholars, archaeologists, and museum professionals in Northern Ireland an opportunity to air their grievances publicly.[5] It is hardly surprising, given the previous examples, that the issue of access to funding intensified competitiveness in many areas and underpinned the entire discussion. The newer interpretative and heritage centers have garnered sufficient funds to avail themselves of the most sophisticated and expensive display technology: the dazzling audiovisuals, holographical displays, dioramic tableaux, etc., designed for maximum sensory impact, and especially appealing to children and younger visitors. In contrast, many of the older and longer established museums and galleries have been stuck with conventional, fusty, even antiquated displays, primarily because of lack of funds. This in turn has fed into the public perception of museums as dull, visually unappealing, or rigidly conservative institutions, criticisms which have been leveled by tourist officials as well. On occasion, museums have also found themselves in the unenviable position of having to provide new heritage attractions with artifacts or professional expertise of various kinds, a situation not calculated to improve relations between them.[6] In the Republic of Ireland debate on these fronts has been complicated and acrimonious. The museum community there has taken Bord Fáilte (the Irish Tourist Board) to task for investing liberally in heritage-related projects while allowing important museums to suffer from insufficient space, inferior display technology, and "piecemeal budgetary arrangements" (Hogan 1993).[7] In turn, the Tourist Board has justifed the large sums allocated to heritage projects by claiming that "tourism understood marketing" and the "heritage for all" concept while the museum sector did not. The latter has, in fact, been charged to "change or else" and to "develop a greater breadth of vision [and] become more people friendly" in order to share in Bord Fáilte's allocation of EC funding, the mainstay of new tourist attractions (Hogan 1993).

In the light of actual quantitative evidence, a degree of resentment on the part of the museum community seems patently justified. The statistics released by the Northern Ireland Tourist Board (NITB) attest clearly that museums play a vital role in the development of cultural tourism in Northern Ireland and the United Kingdom generally (*Museums and Tourism* 1993). In 1992, 7.7 million visits were made to Northern Ireland's visitor attractions, representing a 5% increase over 1991 (NITB Survey 1992:1.1). Visits to Museums and Visitor Centres (a single statistical category) constituted 12% of the overall market share (NITB Survey 1992:1.2). Museums and galleries showed an increase in attendance of 3%, while approximately half of the top visitor attractions in the UK are museums. In fact, museums have experienced greater growth than any other sector for three consecutive years, showing a 10% increase over figures from 1989 (*Museums and Tourism* 1993). NITB statistics further indicate a general shift away from more expensive attractions (which tend to include the newer heritage and interpretive centers), with a 4.5% overall decrease in visits to paid attractions and a 10% increase in visits to free ones, roughly half of which are museums (NITB Survey 1992:1.3).[8] Although investment in the museum sector in Northern Ireland has remained quite small relative to funds invested in heritage centers and other leisure attractions, it has yielded relatively high payoffs (*Museums and Tourism* 1993). Furthermore, the marked stability and vitality of the museum sector in a period of economic recession stands in sharp contrast to the varying fortunes of some heritage and leisure attractions in Britain and Northern Ireland which have in recent years faced abandonment, bankruptcy, or liquidation (*Museums and Tourism* 1993; Runyard 1993:34). Museum professionals would seem quite reasonable in their contention that greater investment in museums, as part of a larger tourism initiative, makes sound fiscal sense.[9]

So museums can and do declaim their strengths: first and foremost, that they offer the public "real heritage", providing a tourism product which combines in-depth research with genuine artifacts; that, as collections-based institutions, they are committed to on-going development and have the potential to deliver constant variety and change; and finally, that they have the combined resources to provide sustainable and varied services. Cultural specialists on both sides of the border weigh in against the whole ambit of "heritage", charging that heritage attractions subtly confuse reality and representation by incorporating both real and simulated "artifacts"; that commercially motivated interpretation is by its very nature fertile soil for the exploitation or distortion of history and tradition; lastly, and more crucially, that spurious heritage continues to be produced as real heritage is neglected or destroyed, issues to which we will repeatedly return.

Ultimately, the issue which looms largest in both public and professional arenas is that of authenticity. The rapid growth of the tourist industry has spawned the entire heritage phenomenon, bringing with it a whole raft of organizations which now compete with museums and other, more traditional institutions in the task of interpreting Ireland's rich and complex past. Stewardship is the essential function of museums, a commission involving interpretation and communication (Hewison 1988:5–6). It entails as well a commitment to authenticity of presentation, while the secondary functions of education and entertainment are to be accomplished in the most comprehensive and historically accurate fashions possible. The "mandate" of the new leisure/heritage attractions, if such there be, shifts from that of stewardship for its own sake to that of providing a "pleasurable experience" of some kind in order to maximize visitor numbers and revenue (Hewison 1988:6). The degree to which these new attractions meet criteria of authenticity must be evaluated very much on an individual basis, for while there a number of superb examples of "interpretation" about, even a superficial survey reveals unevenness, selectivity, and distortion in the treatment of the historical, literary, archaeological, and other aspects of Irish culture they set out to interpret, and a great range of opinion on the "tourism product" in virtually every instance. In this new climate museums have had to work doubly hard to define and communicate the unique nature of their interpretive and guardianship roles within individual disciplines and, indeed, within the larger context of society.

The Ecology of Heritage

It is surely one of the ironies of the entire heritage industry—and one reason it is so difficult to make unilateral decisions about it—that any development can be at once potentially constructive and destructive, and often in very unpredictable directions. Both the center at Navan Fort in Co. Armagh (Navan at Armagh) and The Great Blasket Island Visitor Centre (*Ionad an Bhlastaoid Mhóir*) at Dun Chaoin, Co. Kerry, have opened within the last five years, largely in response to external threats. One raison d'être for the development of Navan was the protection of the mound and the complex of adjacent sites from further encroachment by the limestone quarry to the east which had been operating on a much smaller scale for quite some time (*Navan at Armagh* 1988).[10] But the creation of the center, with consequent increase in foot traffic, has already begun to cause pressure points at the site itself which will require the implementation of environmental protectives.[11] When the Great Blasket island was put up for sale on the international market a few years ago, a local committee was set up for its protection (*Fondúlacht an Bhlascaoid Mhóir*). A complicated legal quagmire resulted when the committee and the Office of Public Works (OPW) jointly attempted to purchase the island. As a compromise, a plan was eventually conceived to build an interpretive center in Dun Chaoin, on the Dingle Peninsula, to promote the language, music, and culture of the area (White 1993). This center opened officially in April 1994 at a cost of £3.8 million, anticipating more than 100,000 visitors during its first summer season (Hogan 1994).

The Dingle Peninsula has long been regarded as a place of outstanding and often spectacular natural beauty. Travelling westward from Dingle town, the wayfarer encounters sparsely settled, open country, with the wildness of the sea everywhere about it. As part of the remaining *Gaeltachtaí* (areas where Irish is the vernacular language), the area retains its links with Irish traditional culture (i.e., the *real* Ireland) and the values and style of life associated with it. As the main gateway to the nearby Blasket Islands, it also figures prominently in the body of romantic literature which chronicles the hardships and rugged endurance of the last generations of Islanders. Dunquin and the peninsula have thus been objects of the tourist gaze and of annual summer engorgement from outside visitors for a long time—but at a manageable level. The projected number of visitors to be lured by the new interpretive center poses some obvious threats to the natural environment of the peninsula, and to the fabric of social life in the area, if maintained for any lengthy period; only time and very careful management will tell. But the situation well illustrates one of the most problematic aspects of "heritage": its potential to damage what it set out to conserve.

Environmental concerns came fully into play in the consternation over the new interpretive centers planned by the OPW in the Republic of Ireland for the Boyne Valley in Co. Meath, Luggala in Co. Wicklow, and at Mullaghmore, in the Burren of Co. Clare, a saga fully documented in the *Irish Times* since it began in 1991. At that time the OPW, goaded by easy availability of EC Structural Funds, implemented plans for the three new centers without benefit of any preliminary environmental impact studies. By deciding to locate these centers in the heart of ecologically unique and environmentally sensitive landscapes rather than on their peripheries, the OPW intended to offer visitors a "window on the world" being interpreted (McDonald 1993b); vehement contention then arose over the philosophical issue behind the OPW's decision. The proposed center at Mullaghmore became the focus of an intense legal battle and considerable public attention, resulting in a protracted, complicated, and bitter dispute between the OPW and the Burren Action Group in which the Burren committee suffered a very costly defeat.[12] (In the end, only the center planned for the Boyne Valley was able to get planning permission to continue building, while the structures built at the other sites were ordered demolished, adding additional costs for demolition and then the restoration of the sites.[13]) Despite the initial legal drubbing, environmentalists gained considerable moral ground, for the whole affair boldly underscored some basic aesthetic and environmental issues central to the heritage debate in a very public arena while serving cautionary notice to government high-handedness, greed, and misplaced intrepidity. Consciousness and contentiousness over the destruction of the urban environment had been germinating for some time as well.

Tourism "Intervention" and the Marketing of Culture

As we have observed, it has always been the landscape of Ireland, and particularly that of the West, with its rugged, panoramic, and unspoiled beauty, and its sense of openness and isolation, that has been projected historically in the tourist literature.[14] It is also the uniqueness of the west, in relation not only to England and continental Europe but to the rest of Ireland as well, that has proved a powerful tool in Ireland's promotion as a tourist destination (Nash 1993:10B). Set against such a rich backdrop of pre-existing associations, the heritage and interpretive centers that have opened in the countryside, such as the Blasket Islands Centre or Céide Fields in Co. Mayo, have begun life with fertile legacies of romantic images amenable to future embellishment, expansion, or exploitation. Furthermore, the economic strategies of tourism have been buttressed in this century by the emotional thrust of Irish political and cultural nationalism, which has been profoundly anti-urban (Lincoln 1993:205).

Paradoxically, the Republic of Ireland has at the same time been very rapidly transformed from a predominantly rural, agricultural country into an unequivocally urban one (Lincoln 1993:215). Since 1926, the total population of Dublin has more than doubled while that of the inner city (the area encompassed by the canals) has decreased from over 250,000 to 100,000 in a steady, consistent decline. After 1966, the rate of suburban expansion increased substantially as Dublin continued to grow from a compact, densely populated city into a sprawling, decentralized metropolis.[15] The country as a whole has been experiencing massive rural depopulation for well over a century (Edwards 1981:232). There are now more than a million people living in greater metropolitan Dublin, representing approximately 40% of Ireland's population (Lincoln 1993:215).

Consistent with this trend internationally, Dublin's "urban flight" also resulted in a general deterioration of the attractions of the inner city and the overall quality of urban life (Lincoln 1993:207). This situation was exacerbated by the Irish government which provided financial incentives for new growth industries located outside the city while allowing many traditional industries upon which Dublin depended to languish.[16] Both local and national governments exhibited a general disregard for the "historic fabric" of the urban environment and an acceptance of the on-going destruction of Dublin's archaeological heritage (Lincoln 1993:204). The designation of Dublin as "European City of Culture" in 1991 provided a number of exciting challenges to the city but underscored these unpleasant realities as well. It is the growth of the tourist industry and the recognition of the marketability of urban heritage that has brought about a change in attitudes toward cityscapes and the built environment generally, at least at an official level (Lincoln 1993:218).

Within the five-year period 1989–93, the active promotion of heritage tourism in the city of Dublin became part of a larger, on-going initiative to double the number of overseas tourists to Ireland (Lincoln 1993:218). It had become clear that despite the strong literary and cultural connections tourists make with the city of Dublin and its environs (American tourists particularly) and the urbanity of contemporary Ireland, Dublin had failed to generate a distinctive imagery of its own. A major problem to be overcome in the promotion of Dublin as a tourist destination was that of the continued dominance of images of the west in characterizations of what is distinctively Irish (Lincoln 1993:219).

Bord Fáilte took a number of steps to accomplish this. It first determined three salient strengths on which Irish tourism should build: the quality of the natural environment, the potential market represented in people of Irish descent, and the richness of Ireland's "cultural heritage" (Lincoln 1993:218). "History and culture" were targeted in the 1989–93 development plan as a major area of potential expansion, with 40% of the funding from the European Regional Development Fund allotted to advance the "tourism product" in this area (Lincoln 1993:218).[17] The Irish Tourist Board then took the additional measure of seeking outside help from a British firm on the most effective ways to promote Ireland's cultural heritage. In one week the consultancy team visited 110 heritage attractions in the Republic. From this frontal assault it was determined that many fell below international standards and suffered as well from a lack of clarity—and considerable duplication—in their messages. More importantly, they concluded that Irish history was too complex to be grasped in toto by the uninitiated visitor (McDonald 1992).

In pursuit of greater simplicity, Bord Fáilte devised a set of five schema around which interpretive programs in the Republic could be based: Live Landscapes, Making a Living, Saints and Religion, Building a Nation, and The Spirit of Ireland. Each was embellished by its own permutation of storylines (e.g., Land and Sea) and applicable to the country as a whole (McDonald 1992), a strategy intended to guide international tourists to an experience of the "real Ireland," including urban environments, and to fulfill their expectations of Ireland as a distinctive travel destination.[18] It was also hoped that the careful targeting and prioritizing of tourism funds would ensure thematic distinctiveness and consistency in Ireland's tourism product, and ultimately avoid replication (McDonald 1992).

As one might expect, Bord Fáilte's "theme" plan has met with many detractors in Ireland generally, largely because of the oversimplification which it seems to guarantee will be built into future heritage attractions. The guidelines have remained in place, however, and their use has been encouraged in Northern Ireland as well. The Irish press now readily seizes upon ironic results of heritage funding and the extraordinary juxtapositions of preservation and destruction to which it occasionally gives rise.[19]

Returning to Northern Ireland once again, the availability of heritage funds seems to have inspired some projects based on the very flimsiest premises or justified by the most tangential relationships to the host environment, developments in Armagh being a case in point. As I have indicated, the city of Armagh was the recipient of close to £9 million by the end of 1994 in the effort to rejuvenate the city and to establish its reputation as "an international tourist mecca" (*Belfast Telegraph* 6 January 1994). An expansive new complex, St Patrick's Trian, incorporates a number of recently restored buildings which offer an array of attractions and services, including the heritage presentations "The Armagh Story" and "The Land of Lilliput."[20] "The Armagh Story," presented in the "interpretive area" of the Trian, outlines the history of the city in a display covering "seven development eras of belief." It focuses on a number of themes which build up to the unifying image of Armagh as a world ecclesiastical capital: the pre-historic period, the Celtic world of *Emain Macha*, the early Christian period (emphasizing the coming and influence of St Patrick and the development of Armagh as a monastic community), the Viking and Georgian eras, and the emergence of Armagh as an ecclesiastical center. As part of its educational function the Trian also mounts exhibitions and maintains a permanent exhibition on the life of St Patrick. Housed in an adjacent structure, "The Land of Lilliput" is advertised as "a child centered fantasy experience" featuring a "spellbinding interpretation" of scenes derived from Swift's *Gulliver's Travels*. It employs state of the art display technology, including tableaux displays, three-dimensional models, and "hi-tech atmospherics" (Trian brochure).

The Trian as a whole is an enjoyable experience involving the highest levels of technological wizardry and sophistication, not the least of which is "Lilliput's" huge and very impressive talking (!) Gulliver. Yet the Trian seems to me a good example of some of the general problems we have already touched upon. A great deal of the history treated in the "The Armagh Story" is common to Ireland generally and not specific to the city of Armagh. In fact, it is "treated" (in varying degrees of detail) in many other attractions in Northern Ireland and the Republic; Northern Ireland's geographical compactness merely heightens the likelihood of replication.[21] Furthermore, the impact of the actual "stories" (i.e. their historical content) seems dwarfed by sensational visual images and the overdrive of the technology. (The Trian features a life-sized figure of architect Francis Johnston narrating "The Armagh Story" from a rafter high above the viewer's head, and the several times larger-than-life Gulliver speaking to a Lilliputian standing on his hand, and to us even further below. Talking and/or severed heads have become a staple of the new heritage attractions.)[22]

It is all very impressive technologically, but there are problems of credibility and misrepresentation here. To begin with, it requires a great leap of faith to accept Jonathan Swift's summer visits to Armagh as sufficient justification for marketing "The Land of Lilliput" and the decidedly *English* Gulliver as "heritage" attractions in Northern Ireland. In addition, everything about the presentation and actual physical layout of the Trian sets up a parity in historical importance between a rather meager Swiftian connection and the entire ecclesiastical history of Ireland—a bald example of the tendency to elevate the trivial at the expense of the important of which heritage attractions have so often been accused ("Saints"). One also gets the uneasy feeling that local authorities must consider foreign visitors either too gullible or too uninformed to detect the misrepresentation involved. This may do considerable injustice to visitors who are very knowledgeable about aspects of Irish culture while contributing little to the delicate kinds of social relationships upon which successful tourism depends.

The interpretive center at Navan Fort in Co. Armagh in Northern Ireland well exemplifies the often extreme difficulty of evaluating heritage attractions in terms of authenticity. Built within walking distance of the foremost archaeological site in Northern Ireland (*Eamhain Mhacha*, "The Twins of Macha"), Navan at Armagh is undoubtedly the premier interpretive center (as distinct from museum) in Northern Ireland in virtually every respect. The building itself is impressive for its very unobtrusiveness: the meadow surrounding the center rises up and over the roof so the structure seems to emerge organically from the undulations of the landscape, the only visible aspects being some dry stone wall and windows to let in light. It was designed to create the illusion that there is no building there at all (Mullan 1995:37). Once inside, visitors find themselves in a spacious, semi-circular vestibule where rich red columns ascend dramatically above a tiled floor, contrasting to the dark greens that pervade the interior. From this point the galleries, educational facilities, and visitor amenities radiate (more or less) outward. Overall the center is highly atmospheric, evoking dim memories of the woods and of the chase and of the romantic and heroic figures who played out their passions in the ancient tales.

Navan's interpretive program is also state of the art, taking the visitor through a carefully constructed three-part sequence (lasting 70 minutes) which uses sophisticated display and interactive technologies to convey both facts and speculation about the history, archaeology, and religious significance of *Eamhain Mhaca* and its complex of related sites and artifacts. It draws heavily upon the two primary sources of information on *Eamhain*: the tangible archaeological evidence and the tales of the Ulster Cycle, stories from the medieval manuscript tradition which intertwine vital socio-historical information with the "fictional" material of myth and legend, and which have found a home in oral tradition as well.

The first segment of the program, "The Dawning," combines an audio-visual presentation with three-dimensional tableaux to introduce visitors to the "wonders" of Celtic Ireland and developments in the early Christian period, including the preservation of the native literary tradition in the monastic milieu, and up to contemporary storytelling. This serves as a prelude to the second stage, or "Realworld," a gallery exhibition involving a range of techniques (interactive computer displays, models, and dioramas) to explain the history and the socio-religious significance of the ritual site and the techniques used in archaeological excavations and research. Most of the artifacts on display here are replicas, including the by now emblematic Knocknashade Trumpet (Mullan 1995:36). In the final segment, the "Otherworld," the sojourner moves into a relatively large amphitheater to view colorful, dramatic, and impressionistic film renderings of several well-known stories from the Ulster Cycle, including "The Cattle Raid of Cooley" (the *Táin Bó Cuailgne*).[23] The entire program is an audiovisual extravaganza, criss-crossing many important facets of archaeology, history, language, and tradition.

The requisite tourist amenities at Navan are also of a very high standard. In addition to the usual tourist knick-knacks and souvenirs, the attractive gift shop sells an interesting range of items Irish and "Celtic," including music and stories from the Navan presentation and other educational materials produced by the Navan Center. The cafeteria-style restaurant is comfortable, spacious, and reasonably priced, offering cuisine definitely a cut above that of many other museums and tourist attractions in Northern Ireland (as I can personally attest). In every respect the structure and its facilities are aesthetically pleasing and well maintained, yet redolent of the unique and mysterious site itself.

Nevertheless, among the compass of my friends and professional associates, reactions to the exhibition at Navan have been mixed. Some feel too much importance has been given to the archaeological section—even that it should be housed in a separate structure. Others observed a lack of encouragement on the part of the center staff to explore the actual physical site or, conversely, expressed concern that it be more adequately protected. Opinions also varied regarding the stories of the "Otherworld" presentation: several parents felt there was too much material to be digested in just one sitting, especially by small children. The music was also considered too dramatic, interfering with an appreciation of the actual stories. On a more serious level, it was suggested that the elimination of the "pillow talk" and the more human-scaled motivation from Navan's specially scripted version of "The Cattle Raid of Cooley" has produced a more baldly political and predatory tale (in the Northern Ireland context) than the medieval manuscript version upon which it is based. Finally, there were those individuals who simply opposed Navan's attempt to streamline and popularize historically important and culturally complex tales.

I advance these criticisms of Navan at Armagh's interpretive program solely to suggest the veritable minefield involved in the creation of a successful "tourism product": the real archaeological and symbolic significance of Navan virtually guarantees that any attempt at interpretation will galvanize a whole range of public opinion. The meanings to be derived from any heritage attraction are neither static nor inherent but must always be arrived at, and this is especially true in Northern Ireland with its conflicted history and cautious present, and where the public generally is so highly sensitized to any suggestion of misrepresentation, sectarian bias, or hidden agendas that even a consensual level of neutrality is almost impossible to achieve. In this sensitive cultural and political context heritage enterprises must proceed with a keen awareness of the possibilities for creating or reinforcing dissonant heritage.[24]

The Tower Museum in Derry presents an excellent example of an institution which has had to face head-on the thorny problem of interpreting the history of one of Northern Ireland's deeply divided communities. The eruption of The Troubles in the late 1960s brought very dark days to Derry, involving the destruction or devastation of virtually thousands of the city's homes and businesses. There followed in the 1970s a massive movement of Protestants out of the city center across the River Foyle and over to the "Waterside," leaving the inner city with an overwhelmingly Catholic or Nationalist population. In the course of the Troubles, thousands have been arrested, detained, or imprisoned, and deaths in Derry account for almost 8% of all the violent deaths due to the Troubles in Northern Ireland since 1969 (Lacey 1993:58–59). Derry's serious political instability has also been compounded by a long history of high unemployment (Lacey 1993:58). Brian Lacey, Director of Derry's Heritage and Museum Service, has argued that city's problems have been caused, at least in part, by inadequate and misguided social policies:

> At least some of the reasons which led to that crisis derived from the inheritance of a controversial, turbulent and religiously and politically divided past. Public policies had inhibited dispassionate study or even awareness of that past, except in a few semi-mythical areas ... which were exploited by those in authority on the respective sides of the community divide for the purposes of ensuring social control and tribal exclusiveness (Lacey 1993:58).

Clearly, the development of the museum was to raise some provocative political questions regarding the role of a museum in a city with this turbulent political history and the relationship of the museum to future economic development and tourism (Lacey 1993:60).

The museum developed initially as one response to Derry's cultural and political crisis. At the time that Derry's Heritage and Museum Service was inaugurated in 1986,[25] the city had virtually no dedicated museum buildings. From the outset the primary concern of the Museum Service was the accurate presentation of the diverse heritage of the city and an interpretation of its history which would have "street credibility" in Derry itself. This required an authentic treatment of the lives of the people who live there, including the negative experiences of the last twenty-five years, as well as some acknowledgment that the people's history generally, both Nationalist and Unionist, had been suppressed (Brian Lacey, personal communication, 24 January 1995). These goals were reflected in the two main items on the Museum Service agenda: to provide a range of visitor facilities which would bring about economic rejuvenation through the development of tourism and to make a contribution to cross-community understanding and reconciliation (Lacey 1993:57). In the ensuing period the Museum Service has gone on to create four museum and display areas within the city, to develop the city's documentary resources, and to organize a variety of special events and outreach programs (exhibitions, lectures, seminars, arts performances, etc.) (Lacey 393:57–58).

The Tower Museum now exists, at least in part, as a symbol of Derry's commitment to a brighter future, but it has not been a battle without obstacles. The Heritage and Museum Service was able to overcome some of the funding limitations to which museums in Northern Ireland are subject (noted above) by including the development of heritage attractions within its brief. But because the bulk of the initial capital outlay for the museum was to come primarily from tourism funding (with the Northern Ireland Tourist Board acting as agent for the European Regional Development Fund), a problem arose when the tourism interests involved opposed any presentation of the negative aspects of the city's history. They opted instead for an interpretive center focusing on the Siege of Derry (1688), perhaps the best known and most crucial event in the city's long history.[26] The Museum Service objected fundamentally to this "fairy tale" treatment of a single historical event, and especially the Siege, which has continued to dominate Derry's history and imagery to the present (Brian Lacey, personal communication, 24 January 1994). The Museum Service was also convinced that a substantial percentage of tourists made their way to Derry precisely *because of* The Troubles there (Lacey 1993:63). Deliberations on these points delayed the project for an entire year.[27] With the backing of the Derry City Council, the Museum Service eventually won out and maintained its original commitment to tell the whole of Derry's story; the other bodies concerned ultimately acquiesced (Lacey 1993:62).

Another controversy arose over the video on The Troubles produced for the Museum by the Heritage and Museum Service because, as we have noted, the Northern Ireland Tourist Board and the Department of Economic Development in Belfast opposed any reference to The Troubles in a tourism context (Brian Lacey, personal communication, 24 January 1994). Although the Derry District Council was fully apprised of what the video would contain at all stages of its development, some of Derry's Unionist councilors were upset with the finished product (Lacey, personal communication, 24 January 1994).[28] In particular, they wanted more emphasis on the Unionist community[29] and some reference made to the massive migration of Protestants over to the Waterside. The video museum visitors now see incorporates changes requested by Derry's Unionist community; the general public never actually viewed the original.[30]

The museum's exhibition, "The Story of Derry," has proved very popular with the public, attracting over 100,000 visitors since its opening (*Insight* 1995). Visitors enter through the O'Doherty Tower to be taken on a straightforward, chronological journey from the prehistoric past ("Origins") to the present ("In Our Lifetime" and "Present Day"). Individual centuries (the sixteenth through the twentieth) are punctuated by dominant historical themes such as the monastic period with the coming of Colmcille, the Plantation, the Siege, emigration, and World Wars I and II, each in its own display area. The exhibition is finished to the highest display standards (Walsh 1993:45), and its narrative line and actual physical layout (with plenty of benches for sitting) combine to create an educational, unhurried, and (by general consensus) a pleasurable museum experience.

"The Story of Derry" continues to receive awards for outstanding professional achievement[31] and has managed to earn wide-ranging support from across

Northern Ireland's complex political spectrum (Lacey 1993:63), no easy feat in itself. Yet a degree of unwarranted triumphalism seems to surround the whole enterprise: one cannot escape the impression that the exhibition ultimately arrived at an acceptable but safe and unchallenging consensus. Nonetheless, the exhibition must be considered for its time and daunting political climate, when "no one would put anything up in Derry" (Brian Lacey, personal communication, 24 January 1994); it was a crucial first step.

There are several other heritage attractions in Northern Ireland which have not been well received in terms of local opinion if not actual visitor numbers. The "Knight Ride" in Carrickfergus (Co. Antrim), which opened in 1993 at a cost of £3 million, is one of the most expensive attractions to be built in Northern Ireland. It was immediately popular with the general public (children especially), bringing in 30,000 visitors within its first year of operation ("Saints") and increasing the number of visitors to Carrickfergus Castle as well. Nevertheless, it remains an object of almost universal derision (at least in casual conversation) and, if not dismissed outright, is invariably referred to as "plastic heritage" or "Disneyesque." What accounts for the scorn the "Knight Ride" provokes?

The Knight Ride is housed in Carrickfergus' new Heritage Plaza, a large, ultramodern structure of steel and glass sporting vibrant, colorful banners inside and out; it stands in sharp contrast to the architecture and generally economically benighted atmosphere of Carrickfergus. Northern Ireland takes its history very seriously, and the Knight Ride—big, bold, and flashy—is just a little startling in this context; certainly there is nothing else quite like it in Northern Ireland. It is clearly an amusement first and a heritage attraction second, whatever the original intention may have been.

Carrickfergus Castle, the other major visitor attraction in the town, is the best preserved castle from the Norman period in Ireland. The decision to build a second visitor attraction in Carrickfergus was part of a much larger plan for economic regeneration which involved the upgrading of the Castle (the flagship of the Department of the Environment's historic monuments in Northern Ireland), waterfront development, general beautification of the town, and the creation of Carrickfergus as "a total heritage environment." The Knight Ride was to provide the complement—Castle cum town—to a total tourist package to be marketed as "Carrickfergus by the Sea" (Development Proposal, DOE NI, 1989).

Billed as "the only monorail themed ride in Ireland—North or South," the Knight Ride promises that patrons will experience over "1000 years of Carrickfergus' exciting history" and "see, feel—and even smell—the past of one of Ulster's liveliest towns" (Knight Ride brochure). For the first part of this journey, the "High Ride," the time traveler steps into a gondola (equipped with stereo speakers) to sail high above Heritage Plaza among colorful representations some of the famous sailing vessels which dominated Carrickfergus' history. The accompanying narrative (by Ulster actor James Ellis) chronicles "bloody naval battles, famous departures, and daring exploits at sea" (brochure). For the second section, the "Dark Ride" (actually a more conventional theme park amusement), travelers move through scenes from the town's history, viewing Norman knights in combat, Carrickfergus' haunted house, and the landing of William III (1690). There are lots of special effects, with music, sights, sounds, and narration—and lots of banging, clattering, shouting and screaming. The final section includes a walk-through gallery containing a scale model of Carrickfergus town (with a soundtrack narrating its history) and a gallery of historical photographs and illustrations. From here travelers are disgorged into the Plaza which has a nice cafe and gift shop, the usual tourist amenities, retail shops, and a Tourist Information Office.

I found the Knight Ride fun and entertaining even though, as a novice to the history of Carrickfergus, it took several trips before I could differentiate the storylines (which are solidly based on local history) from the high-powered audiovisual effects. It is still too early to predict its staying power (in which return visits are crucial), but as a local attraction it has already justified itself on many fronts as well as increasing the number of visitors to the town.[32] The Knight Ride attests to the potential for a range of successful heritage attractions, with different mixtures of history, artifacts, theatricality, and audiovisual trickery, but still meeting the highest possible museological standards—an economic reality Ireland may have to learn to live with.

As a final consideration here we turn to the Ulster American Folk Park in Co. Tyrone. It is one of the most popular tourist attractions in Northern Ireland, but it has also been the object of some of the most serious criticism of *heritage*. Prior to 1994 (when the Emigration exhibition opened), the park was primarily an outdoor museum, somewhat similar to its sister institution, the Ulster Folk and Transport Museum in Co. Down, but with a very different story to tell. Located in a beautiful rural area in Co. Tyrone, the suggested route through the grounds brought the visitor from an Old World setting in the Ulster countryside (with cottages and other reassembled buildings) through a nineteenth century street, and into a gallery area of dockside streets. (Buildings throughout the park were moved and rebuilt brick by brick from different locations in Northern Ireland). In the dock one encounters an emigrant ship, or rather, the reconstructed interior of a nineteenth-century brig (modeled on the *Union*), approximately 100 feet long. The atmosphere of steerage has been carefully recreated with the sounds and smells of crowded living quarters. Visitors then disembark into a New World landscape, a Pennsylvania of maple trees and "log cabins" and peopled with inhabitants engaged in typical household tasks or recounting tales of their voyage. A gallery in the dockside provides a bird's eye view of the ship and dockside scene, and there is an exhibition on the ships themselves (how they were built, sailed, etc.).

In 1994 the Park opened its first major gallery exhibition, "Emigrants—Two

Centuries of Emigration," chronicling the history of the over two million people who left Ulster in the eighteenth and nineteenth centuries. Structured around four major themes ("People and Places," "Failure and Opportunity," "Transport and Migration," and "Survival and Opportunity"), the exhibition investigates the historical causes of emigration, the experiences of the new arrivals, and their contributions to the New World through details of the lives of particular individuals (John Dunlap, Thomas Mellon, and others). The themes are developed through a variety of the most sophisticated media, including detailed dioramas, scanachrome images, period tableaux, audiovisual and interactive computer displays, and a range of original artifacts. Since the opening of the Exhibition, the Folk Park has also hosted a major international conference on the Famine, "The Hungry Stream" (1995), and continues to build up its database on all aspects of Irish emmigration to North America (including Canada) from the 1700s to the 1900s. It has become a major educational and research facility and has also established an annual calendar of events celebrating many aspects of the Ulster-American connection (e.g., July 4th activities, a yearly Bluegrass festival).

As an Irish-American coming from a "Catholic-Nationalist" background (both parents from Co. Cork), I found the very concept of the park surprising on my first brief visit there in 1991.[33] In many subsequent visits I have enjoyed a range of events at the park and have learned a great deal more about this Ulster-American connection. It is this very "foundation myth" of the park which has received so much criticism in heritage commentary. David Brett, in a number of publications, has taken the Ulster American Folk Park to task for what he feels to be its unspoken sectarian premise. Brett argues that the narrative represented by the visitor's journey from the Old World setting of Ulster to the Pennsylvania countryside is not a neutral, geographical one; that it is, in fact, "Ulster-*Presbyterian*-American" [emphasis my own] and "a statement of a distinct cultural tradition" (1993:189). As such it communicates only a partial view of Ulster history, and one which minimizes the appalling economic conditions which caused the largely Catholic mass migrations of the nineteenth century in favor of the voluntaristic movements from Ulster spurred by religious and political idealism (Brett 1993:189). It is not the slant of the narrative of the exhibition that Brett objects to, but the fact that it is not made clear from the start (Brett 1993:89).

Although I have much simplified Brett's criticism and analysis here, his concern lies with the power of heritage attractions to misrepresent and distort history, and he cites the exhibition as an example of the "extension of the power of the manipulated spectacle over history"(Brett 1993:201). In my own experience in Northern Ireland, including the context of tourism, I have seen the "Ulster-American connection" used in a myriad of ways to pervert, distort, or exclude aspects of the larger Irish-American experience (although this connection too is hardly without its problems) in order to advance particular cultural,

economic, and/or political agendas. This complex political situation has only
been intensified in recent years by the enormous influx of European funding
since the ceasefire and, especially, by President Clinton's visit to Northern Ireland in 1995 (and the promises it seemed to hold out).[34]

In this survey I have provided some important examples of the deep inter-
penetration of tourism, economics, and heritage, particularly here in Northern
Ireland where the past cannot yet really be said to be "past", and where its
meanings and cultural implications are very much in a process of delicate negotiation. But heritage points to the future as well as the past. Many areas of
Northern Ireland, and of the Republic as well, have been highly disadvantaged
in many ways for a very long time. What Ireland has, and has had, where heritage is concerned, is an embarrassment of riches, and the tie-in with tourism
plays a very important role in economic development and redevelopment at the
local level. Where tourism and its spin-off industries ("bed and breakfast" facilities, for example) become central in local economies, as they are increasingly, heritage attractions and the finding that supports them represent very
real human aspirations, plans, and labor in towns and villages all over the island; their success or failure means not just a possible loss of Euro dollars, but
the quashing of hopes for more meaningful lives and for the sustained vitality
of often very old communities.[35]

Acknowledgements

Thanks are due to *Causeway Cultural Traditions Journal* for permission to reprint parts of this essay which were published in an article entitled "Fool's Gold:
Filthy Lucre" (Winter 1995).

Notes

[1]Barbara O'Connor notes in *Tourism in Ireland*, "Since the Victorian era Ireland has
been popularly regarded as a place of great natural beauty worthy of the traveler's gaze."
O'Connor also discusses the representations of Ireland and Irish people which have
dominated the literature of tourism (O'Connor 1993b:69, 70–76).

[2]In the tourist and educational brochures I have examined, I have found summer
schools and festivals in the following areas: literature (including "Living Irish Authors"),
theater, language (Gaelic), folklore and oral tradition (including storytelling), journal-
ism, art (including a cartoonists festival), music (including jazz, blues, bluegrass, and
the Irish harp), busking, photography, archaeology, geology, wild life, history, politics,
contemporary issues, a Hugenot festival, and the general melange of subjects designated "Irish Studies."

[3]The Ulster Museum, the Ulster Folk and Transport Museum, and the Ulster-American Folk Park. Local and regional museums are funded by various local authorities.

[4]All three funding programs are administered by the Northern Ireland Tourist Board.

[5]Attractions discussed in this documentary include the Knight Ride at Carrickfergus, St Patrick's Cathedral at Armagh, the new Navan Centre (Navan at Armagh), St Patrick's Trian (which is coupled with the unlikely "The Land of Lilliput"), the Palace Stables Heritage Centre (also in Armagh), the Benburb Heritage Centre (Co. Armagh), the Armagh County Museum, and the Tower Museum in Derry. Among the discussants were Richard Warner (Ulster Museum), Brian Lacey (Heritage and Museum Service), and Aidan Walsh (Northern Ireland Museums Council).

[6]In 1994 the National Museum in the Republic of Ireland refused outright to loan material to several new interpretive centers run by the Office of Public Works (OPW) because they lacked professional curatorial staff. In March 1994 Dr Seamas Caulfield resigned from the OPW steering committee for Céide Fields when the OPW placed an advertisement for manager of the interpretive Centre at Céide stressing management and foreign language skills rather than professional archaeological qualifications. Dr. Caulfield argued that the center needed a professional curatorial staff in order to guarantee state-of-the-art preservation of its artifacts and resources and on-going development based on sound archaeological research. He also deplored the low level of remuneration for the sophisticated skills actually required in the managerial position (*Archaeology Ireland* 1994).

[7]The National Folklife Collection in Dublin, for instance, had been housed in "an old reform school" due to lack of adequate display space (Hogan 1993).

[8]NITB statistics list 23 attractions in the category "Museum/Visitor Centres." Of the ten which do not charge, five are museums (NITB 1992:2.3).

[9]Contention between the museum and heritage sectors seems likely to lessen considerably as heritage attractions figured less prominently in the subsequent Northern Ireland Tourist Board development proposal (*Tourism in Northern Ireland* 1994).

[10]In 1985 an application to extend the quarry east of Navan Fort led to a public inquiry and increased public concern for the mound. It was eventually determined that quarrying should cease as of 30 December 1987. A Feasibility Study was commissioned by the Navan Port Initiative Group (set up in 1987) which then led to the proposal for the interpretive center, Navan at Armagh (*Navan at Armagh* 1988).

[11]The increased number of visitors to the actual site during the summer months tends to halt the growth of grass in those areas where foot traffic is heaviest. The effects of this only show up in winter, when the heavy rainfall turns the areas with insufficient ground cover (particularly the banks and ditches) into muddy, mucky areas, creating problems when teachers with children return to the interpretive center (personal communication, Adrian Stinson and Paul Mullan, 25 January 1994).

[12]This has been a very complicated battle. In February 1993 the Irish High Court forced the OPW to stop building the center at Mullaghmore, but in June 1994, after a number of victories for the Burren Action Group, the OPW was finally granted legal power to build the center, contingent on the acquisition of appropriate planning permission (*Irish Times*, Home News, 9 June 1994). On 23 November 1993, the *Irish Times* reported that legal opposition to the centers had already cost £1.7 million and was continuing to cost £45,000 per week (McDonald 1993a). By the time of the defeat of the Burren Action Group in June 1994, the group was collectively saddled with court costs of more than £100,000, which it plans to appeal to the Taxing Master of the High Court (Collins 1994).

[13]By 1995 the Office of Public Works had become part of a new government department, that of Arts, Culture, and the Gaeltacht.

[14]Barbara O'Connor points out that there is an historical parallel between areas and countries that are represented as places where holiday makers can "engage in carefree play" in a tourism context and a colonial context in which characterizations of areas as "empty space" has justified colonial expansion (O'Connor 1993b:71).

[15]Suburban expansion in Dublin now consumes 1,000 acres of agricultural land yearly (Lincoln 1993:208).

[16]These included textiles, footwear, paper and printing, food and drink, but all traditional industries were affected (Lincoln 1993:207–208).

[17]The plan was to create 25,000 new jobs as well.

[18]The Bord Fáilte commission which produced this report was cofunded by the EC Commission (Lincoln 1993:218).

[19]Frank McDonald, in one of a series of articles on the heritage industry, pointed out that while the tourist board and the Irish government were backing a plan to reconstruct Old Dublin, "Dublin Corporation had just about destroyed what was left of the *real* medieval city...." At the time when a fake motte and bailey were being constructed at the National Heritage Park at Derry Carrig, Co. Wexford (opened in 1987), a real one was being destroyed by a farmer in Kells, Co. Kilkenny (McDonald 1989). Nuala O'Faolain described as a "neat peace [sic] of Soviet rearrangement of reality" the renovation of Lady Gregory's estate in Co. Galway, complete with stables, gardens, and farmyard—but no house. For £500 the Department of Agriculture sold it to a local, who then demolished it (O'Faolain 1994). In March 1996 the remains of the thirteenth-century Augustinian Friary in the Temple Bar area of Dublin were dismantled to allow for a basement burger bar.

[20]The Trian also includes the Rotunda Gallery, the Old Bank House, a courtyard with shop and craft units, the Granary Building, Armagh Ancestry, the Tourist Information Centre, and a car park-all, a multi-service attraction.

[21]Examples can be found at the Tower Museum in Londonderry, the Navan Centre in Armagh, the North Down Heritage Centre, the Down County Museum, Glendalough in Co. Wicklow in the Republic, and the exhibition at the Ulster Museum in 1994, "Patrick: Life and Legacy".

[22]The exhibition "Patrick: Life and Legacy" at the Ulster Museum (1994) had a life-sized animated figure of St Patrick writing his *Confession*. Very realistic decapitated heads can be found in the Tower Museum in Derry and in the Knight Ride in Carrickfergus.

[23]The others are "Deirdre and Naoise," "How CuChulain Got His Name," "The Naming of Navan," and "The Navan Dragon."

[24]*Dissonant* heritage refers to the fact that the same heritage artifact can hold different values simultaneously.

[25]It was created as a subsection of the Recreation and Leisure Department, under the auspices of the Derry City Council. It must be remembered that, with no independent "national" government, the local councils are currently the highest level of government administration in Northern Ireland.

[26]Londonderry has actually withstood three sieges: 1641, 1649 and 1688.

[27]Brian Lacey felt that the Northern Ireland Tourist Board was initially very apprehensive about the possible orientation of the Heritage and Museum Service, fearing that the largely nationalist council would support the production of Catholic/nationalist exhibition at the museum (Brian Lacey, personal communication, 24 January 1994).

[28]*Unionist* in the context of Northern Ireland refers to those wishing to maintain the political 'union' with Great Britain (i.e., wishing to remain part of the United Kingdom).

[29]The councilors wanted more examples of what might be called "Protestant" buildings in Derry (churches, etc.).

[30]The Museum Service agreed that some of these omissions should have been in the video from the outself (Brian Lacey, personal communication, 24 January 1994).

[31]In 1993 the Tower Museum was the recipient of the prestigious Gulbellkian Award. In 1994 the Museum received the UK National Heritage IBM Museum of the Year Award and a second place in the Europe Museum of the Year Competition (*Insight* 1995).

[32]The Tourist Board claims that the increase in visitor numbers to Carrickfergus Castle is a spin-off from the Knight Ride. The Historic Monuments branch of the Environment Service (within Northern Ireland's Department of the Environment [DOE NI], and which owns the Castle) claims just the opposite, that the castle draws them.

[33]I was a participant in the British Council's first "Folklore Study Tour" to Northern Ireland in 1990.

[34]Northern Ireland saw a 67% increase in holiday makers in 1995, the first full year of peace (*Belfast Telegraph* 8 March 1996), and the offer of a £250 million "peace package" from Europe in 1996 (*Belfast Telegraph* 12 March 1996).

[35]1995 saw the demise of "Celtworld" in Tramore, Co. Waterford (Republic of Ireland), one of Ireland's first really "high-tech" tourist/heritage attractions. This represented a loss of £4 million to the investors and a devastating loss to the community.

References

"Around and About" (1994) *Local History Link*. No. 11. The Federation for Ulster Local Studies.

Brett, David (1990) "The Construction of Heritage." *Circa* 53:21–25.

Brett, David (1993) "The Construction of Heritage." In *Tourism in Ireland: A Critical Analysis* (edited by O'Connor, Barbara and Cronin, Michael), 188–202. Cork: Cork University Press.

"Céide Fieldes Row" (1994) *Archaeology Ireland* 8:4.

Collins, Liam (1994) "Burren Group Quits Battle Against OPW." *Sunday Independent*, 7 August.

Edwards, Ruth Dudley (1981) *An Atlas of Irish History*. Reprint edition. London and New York: Methuen.

"Green Light for Visitor's Centre" (1993) *Down Democrat*, 27 October.

Hewison, Robert (1988) "Making History: Manufacturing Heritage?" In *The Dodo Strikes Back* (edited by Iddons, John), 3–9. Twickenham: Strawberry Fair.

Hogan, Dick (1993) "Ireland: An Historical Zoo?" *Irish Times*, 3 March.

Hogan, Dick (1994) "Another Time, Another Place." *Irish Times*, 16 April.

Insight—A Bulletin from the Northern Ireland Museums Council (1995) March.

Irish Times (1994) Home News, 9 June.

Lacey, Brian (1993) "The Derry Museum Service and the Regeneration of the City." *Musuem Ireland* 3:57–63.

Lincoln, Colm (1993) "City of Culture: Dublin and the Discovery of Urban Heritage." In *Tourism in Ireland: A Critical Analysis* (edited by O'Connor, Barbara and Cronin, Michael), 57–63. Cork: Cork University Press.

McDonald, Frank (1989) "When the *Real* Ireland is not Real at All." *Irish Times*, 2 August.

McDonald, Frank (1992) "Variations on a Theme Park." *Irish Times*, Weekend, 19 September.

McDonald, Frank (1993a) "Why Revised Plans for Centres will be Opposed." *Irish Times*, Home News, 23 November.

McDonald, Frank (1993b) "Clearer Vista Ahead for Conentious Visitor Centres?" *Irish Times*, 3 June.

Mullen, Paul (1995) "Where Myth and Reality Meet: Navan Fort and Its Interpretive Centre." *Causeway Cultural Traditions Journal 2(1):36.*

Musuems and Tourism: A Discussion Paper (1993) Northern Ireland Musuems Council.

Nash, Catharine (1993) "'Embodying the Nation'—The West of Ireland Landscape and Irish Identity." In *Tourism in Ireland: A CriticalAnalysis* (edited by O'Connor, Barbara and Cronin, Michael), 86–112. Cork: Cork University Press.

Navan at Armagh: A Feasibility Study (1988) Navan Fort Initiative Group.

O'Connor, Barbara (1993a) "Introduction." In *Tourism in Ireland: A Critical Analysis* (edited by O'Connor, Barbara and Cronin, Michael), 1–10. Cork: Cork University Press.

O'Connor, Barbara (1993b) "Myths and Mirrors: Tourist Images and National Identity." In *Tourism in Ireland: A Critical Analysis* (edited by O'Connor, Barbara and Cronin, Michael), 68–85. Cork: Cork University Press.

O'Faolain, Nuala (1994) "A Richly Satisfying Haven..." *Irish Times*, Home News, 18 August.

Runyard, Sue (1993) "Museums and Tourism in Britain." *Museum Ireland* 3:33–9.

"Saints, Scholars, and Heritage Centres" (1993) BBC Northern Ireland, "Spotlight" documentary series.

Survey of Visitor Attractions—1992 (1992) Research Department. Northern Ireland Tourist Board.

Tourism in Northern Ireland—A Development Strategy, 1994–2000 (1994) Consultative Draft Document. Northern Ireland Tourist Board.

Walsh, Aidan (1993) "Cultural Tourism and Museums." *Musuem Ireland* 3:41–9.

White, Victoria (1993) "Interpreting Without Tears." *Irish Times*, 13 May.

4

TOURISM BEYOND APARTHEID: BLACK EMPOWERMENT AND IDENTITY IN THE "NEW" SOUTH AFRICA

SIMON GOUDIE, FARIEDA KHAN AND DARRYLL KILIAN

> Gone ... are the days when Southern Africa was looked on as a land of unknown dangers, where there was every chance of being killed by treacherous savages. Nowadays the ultramodern and primitive go hand in hand and this is precisely one of the country's greatest charms in the eyes of people from overcrowded older countries (South African Railways and Harbours, 1935).

Introduction

The 1990s have witnessed growing controversy regarding the role of tourism as a vehicle for development in the Third World. Tourism is often promoted as an economic panacea in such regions, its benefits including the generation of foreign currency, the creation of employment, and the diversification of markets. Many Third World governments have been quick to realize the advantages of promoting their countries as tourist destinations at a time when First World markets are becoming increasingly focused upon "wild" and "exotic" holiday experiences. Critics have charged, however, that the industry as a whole offers anything but "quick fix" solutions. Prostitution, drug trafficking, and crime are seen as some of the more obvious and severe problems linked to tourism, but there are also more insidious problems associated with the ways in which traditional cultures are marketed and commodified. For many communities there is the sad reality that the promised benefits of tourism seldom amount to more than mundane, low-paid, and seasonal service jobs instead of real empowerment.

These critiques and debates have particular relevance to South Africa in the post-apartheid era. As the country struggles to come to terms with the tasks of both social and economic reconstruction, there is an obvious temptation to embrace an industry which promises extensive financial rewards. But the history of South Africa points to the urgent need to look beyond obvious financial indicators of success and growth. In the past, few black South Africans were allowed access to the tourism industry, either as tourists, operators or managers; at worst, black cultures were ignored or repressed, at best they became stereotyped and trivialized commodities in the tourism economy. Thus an analysis of the South African tourism market should necessarily be extended to include deeper and more complex social issues of power, access and identity. It should also assess the degree to which the tourism industry can be used to address and challenge the inequities of the past.

Ironically, very little tourism research has been produced in South Africa either before or after the apartheid era. What research has been undertaken has been preoccupied with less pressing issues of standards, the quality of service delivery, and the rating of guest lodges and hotels. Critical research on tourism in urban areas—and black urban areas in particular—remains severely underdeveloped. There is an urgent need, therefore, to address this imbalance in knowledge and to trace patterns of change and transformation. Without rigorous assessment, there is a danger that the South African tourist industry will simply perpetuate past divisions or replicate the negative impacts of tourism elsewhere.

This chapter focuses on three specific issues related to the transformation of the South African tourism market, predominantly within an urban context. First, it examines issues related to empowerment and transformation on an institutional level, mainly within the Western Cape Province[1] (see Map 1), one of South Africa's leading tourist destinations. Attention is also given to the available "points of entry" through which blacks can be trained or registered by existing tourism organizations. Second, the chapter examines issues surrounding the way in which black cultures are now represented and marketed by the formal tourism industry. We argue that despite the professed concern of the state and the private sector for community participation and upliftment, there has been very little substantive change in the tourism industry. Through case examples, it will be shown that many tourist developments are perpetuating romanticized and distorted images of black cultures. While these images may be inaccurate and disempowering, the profit motive makes it difficult to establish meaningful alternatives in the short term. Finally, the chapter examines the issue of tourism development in black areas by means of an assessment of existing and potential operations in Cape Town's townships[2] (see Map 2 indicating the location of some of Cape Town's major townships).

Institutional Change and Challenges

With the demise of apartheid, increasing emphasis has been placed on the role of tourism as a catalyst for social change and healing in South Africa by the state, the private sector, and community organizations. It is a fitting notion given the history of discrimination and disadvantage in South Africa and the course of historical conflict and opposition to the state. Many of apartheid's most successful and brutal achievements were focused on the arena of leisure in general (Goudie, 1993), and tourism in particular. Conversely, the defiance

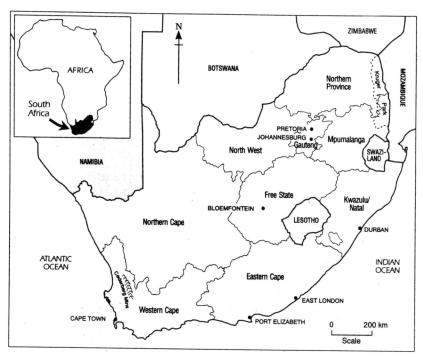

Map 1. National and Provincial Boundaries of South Africa.

of leisure-related laws formed a central part of the national struggle against apartheid, particularly during the 1950s and again during the late 1980s. To achieve social segregation, the National Party implemented a broad range of Acts and ordinances ensuring that different "races" could not come into contact with each other, even in their free time. Almost all infrastructural elements in South Africa were segregated: beaches, hotels, restaurants, libraries, cinemas, parks, camping sites, national parks, post offices, buses and trains, to name but a few; facilities either bore signs indicating that they were for "Whites" or "Non-Whites Only," or the rules of segregation were enforced informally. Locally, such apartheid was often referred to as "petty" apartheid, but it was anything but insignificant or low-key, as this label might imply. It was, instead, an elaborate and humiliating system often entrenched with brute force.

For the state today, the opportunities and reforms possible through tourism thus extend beyond the anticipated economic boom to include a means to promote "political stability....harmony and goodwill" ("Mokaba Taps..." 1994). Necessarily, a program of goodwill as the government sees it includes attempts to promote affirmative action, and to offer practical solutions to overcome the disadvantages that many black South Africans experienced in the past. Thus, as Peter Mokaba, Chairman of the National Tourism Forum, argued in 1994, it is vital to ensure that access to land and credit is made available, as well as ensuring that the old tourism structures and institutions are transformed.

On the ground, however, there is little evidence of a concerted commitment to institutional change. SATOUR (the South African Tourism Board), the national body established by the previous government to promote and market South Africa during the apartheid era, has been particularly slow to demonstrate tangible evidence of transformation. As Parker (1994) argues, SATOUR's commitment to community-driven tourism and affirmative action remains on the level of rhetoric rather than action. Dor (1995) concurs with this argument, adding further that SATOUR remains preoccupied with the needs of the lucrative international market and domestic white market, rather than attending to the needs of those formerly excluded from the industry. Disturbingly, even where "new" tourism boards and organizations have been established after the removal of formal apartheid, such structures frequently use the expertise of those from existing structures, resulting again in a lack of broad representation. The Western Cape Tourism Board, by way of example—the new tourism body reconstructed from the previous Western Cape Tourism Association in 1994—still has only has one black male on its management board (Parker, 1994).

This slow pace of change and the continued First World bias of the industry are starkly evident in the arena of tour guide registration and training, also administered by SATOUR. Out of the 2009 registered tour guides operating in South Africa during 1993, 70% of these were foreign nationals, and only 300 were black (Parker 1994). Registration as a tour guide occurs through SATOUR, as an official state body and standards monitor, while the actual training is undertaken by private colleges. Access to tour guide training at these institutions is prohibitively expensive, ranging between R1000 and R1500[3] for a two week introductory course, and proficiency in English is now a prerequisite. In a country where unemployment is estimated conservatively at 67% in black communities (Central Statistical Surveys, 1994), and with English being a second, third or even fourth language for the majority of South Africans, black exclusion is inevitable. Further, as Parker (1994) contends, with functional illiteracy in black communities bordering on 60%—possibly higher in rural areas—such fees serve as an impenetrable barrier to black participation.

While these current problems of alienation and exclusion are obviously linked to the legacy of apartheid, SATOUR continues to pay little attention to the role of historical forces upon current opportunities; subsidies and support are provided on an ad hoc merit basis. The politically superficial and naive approach of the organization is reflected in the sentiments of McManus, a SATOUR representative, who contends:

> we merely register those that apply and pass the necessary tests...a guide should be knowledgeable... registration takes place on the basis of quality and standards... (cited in Parker 1994).

Training manuals also reflect SATOUR's failure to promote potential market opportunities under the new dispensation. Guides are told that they may not discuss either political or religious topics; and the focus is principally upon beaches, wine farms, and colonial estates and monuments. The word "apartheid" does not feature once in the written guidelines. It is the classic international tourist diet of sun, sea and fun, blended with a dash of colonial elegance. State bodies such as SATOUR seldom market black areas and have made few attempts to investigate or promote the potential of the black tourism market. Consequently, it is not surprising to find—as reported in recent workshop documents in Cape Town's townships—that black residents either did not know what the function of SATOUR was, or regarded it with suspicion and hostility (4U Development Consultants 1995).

The task of transforming the South African tourism market, and encouraging black participation on an institutional level remains further obstructed by a lack of proactive central government initiatives to address the racial inequalities of the past. The recently drafted Green Paper on Tourism tabled in parliament this year (Department of Environmental Affairs and Tourism 1995) suggests a serious commitment on the part of the new government to promote "tourism development and entrepreneurship among communities and individuals of disadvantaged backgrounds" (ibid.:7). But while laudable in principle, central government has yet to offer specific mechanisms to allow black communities access to skills training, capacity building and financial support. With a legacy of minimal basic business management and marketing skills, this will mean, inevitably, that black communities and entrepreneurs will find it difficult to compete against the already well-established and powerful (mainly) white companies in South Africa. Increasing state emphasis on privatization and steady annual reductions in the national tourism budget are additional factors aggravating the difficult task of establishing equitable partnerships. Tourism research in the Third World suggests that private-sector driven tourism developments are seldom associated with real community empowerment (see, for example, the numerous case studies documented in the resource book titled *Tourism and Indigenous People* (Ecumenical Coalition on Third World Tourism 1995)). Many of the problems associated with this sector are exacerbated by the laissez faire approach adopted by governments to attract foreign investment. For South Africa, these international trends suggest that a reliance on private-sector driven reconstruction and reform should be treated with caution, at best as a piecemeal solution.

Heritage Tourism and Identity in the New South Africa

Thus far we have briefly examined change and empowerment trends within the major state organizations that are linked to tourism development, marketing and guide registration in the Western Cape Province. The state, we have contended, has demonstrated few signs of proactive intervention in the tourism market; options for black entrepreneurs wishing to compete in a strongly white and foreign multinational-dominated industry remain extremely limited. We have also argued that there is a pressing need to focus on black culture, changing it from its present marginalized and neglected position to that of a major component and product-base in the tourism market.

The recognition and acceptance of the need for change, however, are only the first links in the chain of reconstruction; specific agendas and market strategies are more difficult to define. Attempts in South Africa to build new commercial packages and products based on black traditions and histories are inevitably fraught with painful political questions and paradoxes. Ethnicity, for example, remains a particularly problematic question in the "new" South Africa, having been the foundation of the previous government's policies of social division and separation. Is the promotion of ethnic and cultural identities in tourism publicity and promotion simply a perpetuation of apartheid agendas, or can it truly be seen as a liberating alternative? Richter (1995:81) cogently observes that while tourism is often marketed as a "politically neutral" domain of human activity, it is characterized by the same complex social faultlines of class, race, and gender that run throughout society. "How we choose to remember and commemorate events," she writes, "is a very political act." This section, examines issues related to black culture in the heritage tourism industry and assesses some of the key problems associated with the reclamation of black identity as a sustainable and possibly profit-generating product.

Reclaiming the Invisible Past

According to the last population census in which "racial" analysis was still undertaken, black South Africans constituted 83.6% of the total (Central Statistical Services 1994, based on the 1991 study). The obvious market potential of a market of this size, combined with the diversity of potential cultural products, suggests that the heritage of black South Africans could—and should—constitute a significant part of the existing tourism industry. However, while there is increasing interest in this heritage sector, it is evident that the legacy of the apartheid past remains a major stumbling block to realizing market potential. Part of this legacy has been the continuance of politically conservative tourism structures that have yet to undergo substantive change. There is also the more serious problem of the conspicuous neglect of heritage sites related to black history. Not only has a romanticized Afrikaner mythology, along with its icons and monuments, been allowed to dominate the South African cultural landscape in the past, but the entire subject of heritage has been dominated by a Eurocentric approach which allowed a distorted and one-sided picture of black cultural heritage to emerge (Khan 1992). This was not surprising given the

racially based power structures of the apartheid era which enabled the dominant white group to impose their ideological bias on the representation of heritage.

Much of the cultural infrastructure of South Africa, such as monuments and
museums, reflects the needs and interests of the white minority, focusing on
aspects of colonial heritage rather than offering a more diverse and sensitive
portrayal of South African history. Bigotry and antagonism towards blacks have
been an integral part of the development of Afrikaner heritage structures such
as the Voortrekker Monument in Pretoria, built to commemorate the migration
of Dutch settlers into the South African interior. A guide book to the monument, for example, informs visitors that:

> The design of the Voortrekker Monument ... was to serve as a tangible tribute to
> a group of people who, through their efforts, had laid the foundation for a white
> civilization to be built in the interior of Southern Africa ... the statue of the
> Voortrekker Mother and her children symbolizes white civilization while the black
> wildebeest portrayed the ever threatening dangers of Africa (Moerdijk 1970:36).

Significantly, this migration of Dutch settlers was triggered by an unwilling-
ness to accept the emancipation of slaves in the Cape Province in 1838. This
imposing fort-like structure which dominates the skyline of Pretoria, is but one
of many monuments and shrines located throughout the country marking this
colonial migration. In contrast, the authors are aware of only one stark and
simple monument in South Africa to celebrate the actual outlawing of slavery.
Alexander (1991) estimated that little more than 2% of all national monuments
are explicitly dedicated to black culture and history.

Despite this heritage of apathy and disregard for black histories, the situation is undergoing rapid and dynamic change. Community organizations and
museologists are now attempting to correct existing racial and cultural bias,
and there have been a number of exciting and groundbreaking initiatives. These
include the National Monuments Council declaring the house of Sol T. Plaatje
a national monument. Plaatje was a noted author, editor and secretary of the
South African Native National Congress, which later became the African National Congress. The house, which now contains a museum on the man and his
life, is the first museum in South Africa dedicated to the memory of a black
person. Another example of change in the heritage tourism industry is the Kwa
Muhle museum in Durban, which is housed in the former Department of Native[4] (later Bantu[5]) Affairs. Depicting scenes of daily experiences of township
and working life, the museum also offers rare insights into the histories of political trade unions and cultural organizations under apartheid, and a documentation of the common history of residents in Durban. A monument was also
erected in 1992 in the township of Soweto, near Johannesburg, in memory of
thirteen-year-old Hector Peterson and other young people who died during the
uprisings of 1976. And recently, Museum Africa was established in Johannes-

burg to re-awaken interest in forgotten aspects of southern African history from pre-colonial times to the present (Powell 1994).

While in the past few parks or reserves acknowledged the early settlement of these areas or offered any interpretive explanation of the culture and way of life of the original inhabitants, today many of the national parks and reserves which form an important part of the tourism industry, emphasize the importance of former black land management practices in these areas. Archeological work is now being carried out on the gold smelters of Thulamela in the Pafuri area of the Kruger National Park (located in the Northern Province; see Map 1). At the Thulamela site, which dates back to the fifteenth century, ruins, pottery fragments and gold beads have been found. There is evidence that this site was not only a gold site but also an important trading and metal smelting center. With its more holistic approach to conservation, the National Parks Board is proving willing to integrate the cultural heritage elements unique to each park into a total ecotourist experience ("Khaditshwene" 1992; "Gaditshwene" 1993).

The task of promoting an awareness and appreciation for black cultures and traditions is not an easy task for those in the tourism industry. Most obviously, this is because much of South Africa's past is tainted by political conflict and violence. There are important and often unsettling questions that arise concerning the degree to which such histories can (and should) be incorporated into a commercial industry. More significantly there is a constant and precarious balance between the need for market sustainability and the need for political integrity—the two not always being compatible. Does one, for instance, run the risk of alienating tourists in search of a wild and exotic "African paradise" by providing them with a diet of "unpalatable" political detail? If black histories are to be incorporated within the mainstream heritage tourism industry, how is this to be achieved without compromising the integrity of both the past and the present? Appealing to the romanticized expectations of tourists may be a profitable exercise but, as Urry (1990) cautions, there is an inherent risk of creating simplified and politically sterile spectacles of local culture.

The task of promoting heritage tourism that acknowledges black cultures is further aggravated by the sheer costs of establishing new tourist markets and sites of interest. These sites, it has been shown, are mainly restricted to white areas; where black participation in the tourism industry does occur it typically takes the form of low level service provision in the employ of white entrepreneurs, in mainly white areas. Such bias is difficult to break. Under the system of apartheid, black South Africans were treated as temporary sojourners within cities; black residential areas were typically characterized by stark alienating environments with little or no infrastructural investments. Many townships in South Africa are relatively new, still separate components of the urban landscape, formed as a result of deliberate segregationist policies and populated by people who had often been forcibly removed from other areas. Thus, in addition to the obvious biases in funding for the declaration and preservation of national monuments, there is the reality that many of the physical elements of black heritage have been actively destroyed (Khan 1993). Today many South African towns are characterized by classic apartheid polarities—two (sometimes three) major nodes built for different "population groups," but with only the white residential and business districts having good infrastructure, services and amenities. Many of the most prosperous tourist towns in South Africa contain lesser known "black areas"—many hidden from sight—which are largely divorced from the industry except insofar as they provide service industry labor. This is a tragic situation, given that while many black sites of interest have been abused or neglected, there are still many that warrant preservation and care.

Thus the task of rectifying imbalances in the heritage industry and promoting black empowerment is not simply that of drawing in established infrastructural elements or tapping into existing black entrepreneurial skills. Rather, those in the tourism industry are faced with the far more daunting challenges of creating a whole new sector of the industry, virtually from the beginning, and rectifying the cost of previous distorted funding practices. Tunbridge (1984:173), reflecting on issues of cultural conservation both internationally and within South Africa, rightly suggests:

> ...there are difficulties of interpretation with minority and disadvantaged groups. In line with their economic status, their material heritage may be quite humble and so not be perceived, let alone respected, by politically dominant groups. In addition, minorities [or those without full political power] are commonly ... occupiers of pre-existing structures to which they have experienced a relatively short period of attachment. In confronting these difficulties, it is necessary to remember that structures of heritage significance are continuously being created. Many that already express the culture and identity of minorities have yet to acquire distinction in the eyes of others, being relatively recent adaptations of pre-existing buildings with or without prior heritage significance.

Current reductions in state funding for heritage sites and museums have aggravated the difficulties of black heritage tourism development. In Cape Town, for example, the District Six Museum in Cape Town, which documents the history of black forced removals from Cape Town's central districts to outlying suburbs in the late 1960s and early 1970s, is already faced with the possibility of closure. Although the museum has received extensive community support and international recognition, decreased state subsidies are already a threat to a project barely two years of age.

Representations of Identity and History

Tourism research reflects increased attention upon the social impacts of tourism on local communities, particularly marginalized indigenous groups. One of the more contentious debates that has arisen as part of this growing consciousness, is centered upon the ways in which cultures and histories are represented and commodified in the tourism market. Urry (1990) contends that the process of creating a commercial tourism product from local cultures, involves a careful selection—as well as the screening—of cultural elements; such products are never simple mirror images of reality. In England, as Urry suggests by way of example, the generation of a romantic rural landscape as a backdrop to the tourism industry, has involved the elimination of historical (and contemporary) features which do not fit comfortably with this bucolic vision. These include "farm machinery, laborers ... concrete farm buildings, motor ways, derelict land, polluted water, and more recently nuclear power stations" (Urry 1990: 98). A constant struggle, he argues, has emerged between market viability and authentic representations of local cultures resulting frequently in a commercial (and political) screening and packaging of reality. What tourists are guided through, Urry suggests, are more often than not profitable "pseudo-events" (Urry 1990:7) reflective neither of past or present realities.

The manner in which indigenous histories have been commodified raise similar important questions in South Africa about power and access in the tourism industry. Black alienation and exclusion from mainstream tourism—both past and present—has meant that most black South Africans have lacked control over the way in which their diverse cultures have been portrayed. Although the industry is undergoing change and transformation, current trends at some of the country's leading tourist attractions suggests that attempts to break with past patterns of distortion and stereotyping may not be so easy. This section examines two of the country's leading tourist attractions, namely Kagga Kamma in the Cederberg Mountains (see Map 1) and the Victoria and Alfred Waterfront development in Cape Town (see Map 2). Particular attention is given in this section to the debates of cultural (mis)representation in tourism and the compromise between commercial viability and historical accuracy that characterize these developments.

Kagga Kamma, a small cultural village and accommodation center, is located in the Cederberg Mountains approximately 200 km north east of Cape Town (See Map 1). In early 1991, three white entrepreneurs decided to "reintroduce" the Bushmen or San people[6] to the area. The San people had originally been displaced from the area in the eighteenth century by colonial migrations and conflict with other indigenous communities into the interior, and had moved steadily northwards into the Kalahari desert. One of many cultural villages now established in South Africa, the objective of Kagga Kamma was to preserve San culture and to raise awareness of a community which had become increasingly marginalized, poverty-stricken and politically powerless.

But the development's achievements and ability to realize these objectives in a sensitive and appropriate manner is highly questionable. Images of San culture promoted at this resort are those of an Eden-like innocence, "the familiar portrayal of Bushmen as Paleolithic foragers isolated from the passage of progress" (White 1993). Here tourists come to see "the last surviving Bushmen" in an "authentic Bushmen settlement." The lure of Kagga Kamma, as Rassool

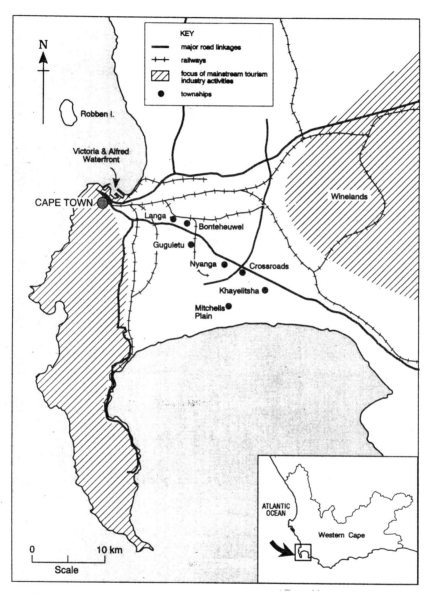

Map 2. Cape Town and Environs: Key Tourist Areas and Selected Townships.

and Witz (1994:24) note, lies in a deceptive and romanticized version of Bushman culture which the tourist is made to feel "privileged to encounter." But there is a deep irony in observing Bushmen in loincloths demonstrating bead work and arrow-making when in fact these traditions have little if anything to do with the experiences of the surviving Bushmen before they arrived at Kagga Kamma. In their displaced existence in the Kalahari Desert—their previous home—the majority of their traditions and skills had been lost and many Bushman had become alcoholic.

Out of sight of the tourists, the San people of Kagga Kamma wear ordinary clothes, buy their food at a shop, send their children to school where they are taught in Afrikaans, and swim in a chlorinated pool. Receiving only a small percentage of the takings of all tourists fees, clan leader Dawid Kruiper is adamant that they are not forced to perform for tourists. The reality is that for a dispossessed people for whom this is one of the only sources of income, the perceived freedom of choice borders on illusion. Indeed, it is hard to avoid the perception of the Kruiper Clan as some form of natural curiosity, a human equivalent of a "Jurassic Park" project. Since their arrival at the Kagga Kamma Resort, the Kruiper Clan have been paraded as a living exhibit at local tourist offices in Cape Town as well as at a major tourist trade exhibition (Neill 1994)—where they took first prize as the best stand! They have also been put on display as part of an ecotourist exhibition in the North West Province, having been brought there by a white tourism entrepreneur as part of a cultural "awareness" experience (Beaver 1996). Such displays where (mainly European) tourists photograph the Bushmen, point, poke and gasp in awe, are alarmingly reminiscent of Victorian exhibits where indigenous people were displayed as curiosities and freaks.

Kagga Kamma is, however, one of the few opportunities for tourists to be exposed to San culture even in a corrupted form and cannot be dismissed outright. A clan member at Kagga Kamma reasons:

> The tourists have never met people in skins, so it's a miracle for them. The day we put on [Western] clothes, they will stop coming. If I go back to the farms I have to put on clothes to work, and then I get little money (cited in White 1993).

On one hand, therefore, the development can be seen as one of the only short term strategies to raise awareness of vulnerable communities. Looking beyond the blatantly racist elements of this project, one can argue that a cultural village like Kagga Kamma is one of few alternatives to an otherwise even more marginal existence.

Further, as Urry (1990) reasons, while certain tourist events and commodities may appear inauthentic and insensitive, they should be understood as products of an ongoing collision between different cultures and a constant negotiation over representation and meaning. As Douglas writes in his discussion of racial stereotypes (1996):

> It is easy to criticize the way in which most hotel and lodge managements have responded to the new trend [in cultural tourism]. Having grown up in a society where blacks and whites were fiercely separated for years ... it [is] difficult for some tour operators to understand African culture, let alone create structures to experience authentic African life.

But, on the other hand, as White (1993) warns, one should not lose sight of the fundamental imbalances of power in the tourism industry. "As long as their lives are shaped in a world beyond their control," he writes, "and around an image of themselves that is not of their own making and that they are unable to manage to their own benefit—[the San] seem destined to remain there." Many of the ecotourist ventures in South Africa in which indigenous people are currently involved, are initiatives like Kagga Kamma, launched by private game lodges or government-owned national parks. However well intentioned, such an enterprise with a powerful senior partner who has probably initiated, funded and implemented the project, is inherently unequal.

A second important example illustrating the controversies in South Africa's heritage tourism industry is that of the Victoria and Alfred Waterfront redevelopment in Cape Town. Now recognized as one of the country's most successful tourist attractions, the Waterfront development is visited by over 12 million people per year (Victoria and Alfred Waterfront (V&AW) Company Information Center, personal communication). This development has proved to be an extraordinary commercial success and is regarded as a major economic engine for Cape Town in particular, but also for the broader development needs of the Western Cape Province. Critics however remain skeptical, arguing that this success has been achieved at the expense of local cultures and communities. They contend that the commercial package of images that underpins this development reflects neither the realities of Cape Town today or those of yesteryear.

For David Jack, Managing Director of the V&AW Company, existing waterfronts internationally were an admitted model for the Cape Town development. According to him, they had succeeded because they had created the "authentic" and "natural" feel of a downtown dockland area (see Kilian 1994). In an attempt to minimize risk, the planners of the V&AW Company opted for the profitable tried-and-tested combinations of postmodern styles and forms—a postmodern "package of plans" rather than attempting new forms tailored to, or reflective of, Cape Town's unique cultures. Like the waterfronts of Sydney, Baltimore and others—tourists in Cape Town experience an almost identical postmodern reconstruction of the past. Pleasant wooden promenades, wrought iron and wooden street furniture and emporium facades invite the visitor to partake in a neo-Victorian life of privileged leisure. The entire Waterfront experience is meant to evoke a sense of wonder and nostalgia, the Victorian age being seen as a golden era of prosperity, carnival fun, romance and spectacle. Such sentiments are clearly reflected in the V&AW Company's award winning audio visual presentation:

> The city was the sea—the sea was the city. The city left the sea—it crept inland, it left the harbor to itself ... it left behind some of the most beautiful buildings, romantic places ... left behind the slap of water, the creak of rope, the groan of wood ... yet today a clock is being carefully turned back ...

This Victorian leisure-world, like others in docklands across the world, is far from being a true reflection of local cultures. What is presented is a sanitized and carefully reconstructed history; the lives of black dockworkers, slaves, convicts, beggars, and others whom made up the social fabric of everyday life in early Cape Town, lie buried beneath these depthless and romanticized images. Worden (1992) one of many vocal opponents to the postmodern waterfont package, challenged the V&AW developers to recognize and present the uniqueness of local cultural landscapes, arguing that the tourist package needed to acknowledge simpler, plainer and no less significant narratives of the mostly black working class communities once (and still) located there.

To dispel perceptions of white exclusivity, the V&AW Company has set about implementing strategies aimed at promoting the Waterfront to a larger black audience. Apart from bussing in underprivileged black children from townships for excursions and educational activities (Ozinsky, personal communication), the company has also, more recently, produced and installed information boards outlining important historical events and figures related to the Waterfront (Bickford-Smith and Van Heynigen 1994). These boards relate the stories of the convicts, slaves and dockworkers who represent the "real" history of the Waterfront and form an important part of integrating black cultural landscapes into the mainstream tourism industry of South Africa. Visitors can now "discover" that the docklands were the site of South Africa's first segregated residential compounds, and were thus an important step in the social progression to apartheid. Photographs of early labor leaders and scenes of Cape Town's eighteenth- and nineteenth-century docklife are also on display.

Finally, we would argue that the Victoria and Alfred Waterfront in Cape Town is also an important example of the tourism industry's reluctance and inability to incorporate current working class black realities into tourism markets. From its inception the V&AW Company has promoted the Waterfront development as a unique "working harbor," combining both tourist activities with existing port related functions. As Brian Kantor, chairman of the V&AW Board reasoned, a "premise—an indeed a condition of the V&AW development ... [was] that the activities of the harbor, mostly fishing related, ... would not only be permitted but encouraged as part of the attraction of [the] Waterfront" (V&AW Company 1991). However, while the company professed to want a "working" waterfront image, they found it increasingly difficult to merge heavy port related industries—often noisy, smelly and hazardous—with the glitz and glamour of the postmodern package. Thus as the Waterfront core has expanded and developed, so the mostly black inshore fishing community have come under increasing pressure to rationalize their operations and relocate to more remote areas, in order to free up water's edge space for more profitable and aesthetically appealing luxury moorings and cruise launches.

For Roy Bross (pers comm), secretary of the Port of Cape Town Fishing Industry Association (POCTFIA), the V&AW Company's attempts to confine fishing activities into ever smaller and more remote areas of the docklands was a reflection of their desire to reduce the size of low status land uses (such as fishing) in favor of superior forms of property development related to the neo-Victorian postmodern tourism package. This increased displacement of black workers is particularly ironic in the context of the Cape Town Waterfront given that initially the working harbor elements were to be a unique component of the development. Van Rooyen (1991:65), in a publicity brochure advertising the new waterfront, argued that this combination of elements would add an unusual charm to the development, "extra zest to the [already] colorful and exciting environment." This example—one of the only explicit attempts to include current urban black working culture in the tourism industry—does not bode well for the commodification of black heritage in mainstream tourism, given the ease with which it has been displaced.

Township Tourism in Cape Town

Thus far we have briefly examined some of the issues of black empowerment and identity within tourism institutions in the Western Cape Province. We have also assessed the representations of black identity and culture at two premiere South African tourist destinations. A key component of apartheid planning was the deliberate segregation of space and the underdevelopment of black areas. Part of this planning strategy included deliberate underinvestment in these areas and the concomitant concentration of superior infrastructures and services in white suburbs and business districts. Like other economic sectors, the tourism industry today continues to reflect this disproportionate bias, with the majority of the tourism industry's infrastructure and attractions being located in, or close to, formerly white areas. A question that needs to be asked, therefore, is whether and how tourism can be promoted within these black areas in order to promote a more integrated society and economy? In this section we focus specifically on initiatives which have been undertaken in black townships, specifically those in Cape Town.

An examination of black tourism in Cape Town is particularly appropriate. As mentioned earlier, the Western Cape Province, and Cape Town specifically, are amongst South Africa's top tourism destinations capturing an estimated 630,000 international visitors per year as well as approximately 726,000 domestic tourists (SATOUR estimates, unpublished). Cape Town is also one of the country's clearest examples of an apartheid city: residential areas have been carefully separated by open spaces, industrial buffer zones, railways and roads. An assessment of change and integration in this region provides an important barometer of the degree to which the tourism industry is attempting to spread its financial and social benefits to black communities previously discriminated against.

Interviews with companies undertaking tours in black areas, revealed that despite the rapid growth of tourism in the broader Western Cape region, growth in this sector is significantly slower.[7] While there are over two hundred Western Cape-based tour operators registered, and while multi-national companies are becoming an increasingly dominant force in the tourism market in Cape Town, there are still less than twelve companies offering excursions into the city's black townships such as Langa, Nyanga, Bonteheuwel, Crossroads, Mitchells Plain, Guguletu and Khayelitsha (see Map 2). Significantly, even these tours are far more small scale than the large commercial bus tours offered on main tourist routes. Transport typically takes the form of a microbus accommodating no more than fifteen people at a time. What then accounts for this lack of growth given the potential tourism markets that could be developed in these areas?

The Spatial Design of the Apartheid City

Interviews revealed that the black townships in Cape Town are marketed as a largely exclusive and separate segment of the tourist experience. Eight of the ten companies interviewed focused specifically on the township market and generally did not incorporate other major tourist sites (in white areas) as part of their itinerary. Township tour operators were unanimous in their concern that many independent and multi-national tourist companies either ignored black areas in their tours, or, at best, mentioned them peripherally. Partly, this fragmentation of the tourist market can be ascribed to the spatial layout of Cape Town as an apartheid city. Under apartheid planning, the city's transport system formed part of the apparatus of segregation, with each mode of transport and its associated infrastructure acting as a means to separate population groups in separate residential areas. Transport infrastructure was also designed in a radial pattern, each line leading to a specific, racially segregated zone. The majority of blacks in Cape Town were also forcibly relocated to peripheral residential areas far from the city center, making casual contact between population groups extremely difficult. People would be able to drive past "other" residential areas, but would not enter them unless they consciously wished to do so.

Part of the reason for the current fragmentation of the tourism industry, and the tendency for black areas to be promoted as a separate market niche, lies in the actual geography of the apartheid city, with the large distances between white and black areas, and the restricted points of access. However, this explanation fails to address the reality that a tourism market fragmented in this way, only serves to perpetuate the social divisions which South Africa needs so desperately to overcome.

Emphasis on Existing Infrastructure and Service Standards

The underdevelopment of black areas as tourism sites can also be linked to the current preoccupations of planning authorities in Cape Town. A key component of the city's strategy to position itself as a major player in the international tourism market involves the deployment of resources to assess the needs of foreign visitors and their perceptions of existing facilities and service standards. Indeed, the production of reports and surveys on these topics have become alarmingly frequent and repetitive. In contrast, far less attention has been given to strategies aimed at establishing black areas as competitive tourism nodes, with such reports typically characterized by operational details on how these areas will become part of the larger Cape Town tourism market, or how residents could participate above the level of service providers, drivers, and cleaning staff.

With Cape Town presently bidding for the 2004 Olympics, black areas have been specifically targeted as potential sites for the siting of a number of sporting facilities. But the degree to which such undertakings can stimulate broader tourism development in areas with little or no other tourist infrastructure is debatable. A spokesperson from the Cape Town City Council (CCC) noted that the reconstruction of black areas as tourist destinations is unlikely to become a planning priority in the short to medium term. Instead, much of the resources and efforts that local authorities are expending, he argued, are concentrated on existing infrastructure with a view to making existing tourist assets more marketable in the lucrative international market (CCC, personal communication, 1996). In the light of the history of South Africa and current socio- economic / spatial inequalities, it is a serious weakness within the tourism industry that the industry's potential as a tool for economic empowerment and social integration has not been fully realized. Black areas, as we have argued, have largely been terra incognita for the tourism industry and, consequently, black South Africans have been given little opportunity to participate as partners or leaders within this industry sector. Without extensive promotion and publicity it is likely that these areas will remain excluded and potential market demands will be unrealized.

A current danger, as 4U Development Consultants—an agency involved in tourism planning and awareness campaigns—contends, is that tourism interventions within the townships are fragmented and uncoordinated. Frequently, when powerful business interests make forays into the townships to assess market potential and establish contacts and initiate tours, these campaigns are poorly linked to a representative cross-section of the community. Proposed training schemes have often been cancelled without explanation (4U Development Consultants 1995). There have also been instances where unregistered training organizations have produced township guides "with no accreditation and therefore lacking in legitimacy and possibly competency" (ibid.:35). These factors combined with the lack of awareness regarding the potential of tourism by local residents and a climate of suspicion regarding outside—particularly state—tourism organizations such as SATOUR, aggravate the difficulties of redefining the townships as tourist markets and emphasize the need for a broad and coordinated strategy from the tourist industry.

The Search for New Images

South Africa has undergone a major transition to democracy, heralding a new era of potential peace and stability. Nevertheless, the country's past continues to limit its development potential today. Crime has replaced political instability in many people's minds as the key factor limiting growth in the tourism industry. As Peter Mokaba, Executive Chairman of the National Tourism Forum, claims ("Mokaba Taps..." 1994:6): "Endemic crime and violence has [*sic*] not inspired tourism confidence. Peace and security are necessary requirements for any successful culture of tourism." Many black townships, in particular, have suffered from perceptions of being places of violence and squalor. While there are undoubtedly still many social problems within these areas, there are also marked variations in safety and standards of living.

Township tour companies in Cape Town, when interviewed, were unanimous that the mainstream, formal tourism industry showed a reluctance to operate in these areas owing primarily to the perceived lack of safety and security. They argued that this is a stereotype of township conditions and that potential risks are significantly reduced by active community participation in the tourism planning process, and by making residents aware of the benefits of tourism to their daily lives through education and training. Seven out of the ten companies surveyed contend that where mainstream (mainly white) tour operators had encountered hostility or indifference, such problems were linked to a lack of sensitive planning and cognizance of local conditions. One township tour operator also contended that the tourist industry needs to adopt new and more flexible strategies. To integrate townships into mainstream tourism, she reasoned, tour operators must adopt more flexible itineraries, going elsewhere if necessary to avoid areas of conflict, or changing the times and duration of their tours depending on the safety and security conditions in townships, which vary day-to-day. This was not to suggest that the problem of crime should be ignored, she argued further, but rather that it should be recognized as a problem not endemic to township areas and an inadequate reason to justify the current lack of investment and interest.

The task of establishing a sustainable township tourism industry will also be dependent on extensive capacity building and training. Traditional ceremonies, traditions, crafts and skills are the basis of a potentially lucrative new industry both for communities and tour operators. But the pervasive reality of discrimination and disadvantage has meant that most black South Africans lack even a basic familiarity and understanding of entrepreneurial skills. In one instance, where a tour operator established contact with a local artist and encouraged her to produce and sell her crafts to visitors, the operation went particularly well, with over R2000 of sales being realized in a single afternoon. A subsequent tour revealed that the seller had taken the money and left, believing it to be a once-off windfall rather than a sustainable source of income. She had left Cape

Town to return to her rural home to share the money with her relatives, and the tour operator was unable to find another supplier of art products that day. This example suggests that the establishment of township tourism projects is more complex than simply identifying new markets and drawing in participants from local communities. What is needed is a longer, slower, and perhaps more costly intervention aimed at building an awareness of opportunities. This may appear to be a more cumbersome and less appealing approach, but without such detailed interventions, the possibility of establishing equitable and sustainable partnerships remains remote.

Conclusion

This chapter has examined some of the key debates and controversies related to the inclusion and empowerment of black South Africans in the tourism industry. While the tourism industry has been recognized both locally and internationally as a substantial and attractive economic sector, problems have also been identified with regard to the representation and participation of indigenous communities, especially in Third World countries. For South Africa, these disputes and allegations have particular resonance as the country attempts to rectify the legacies of apartheid. Black empowerment necessarily extends beyond attempts to promote more equitable business partnerships to include finding new ways to address the neglect and misrepresentation of black cultures. Kagga Kamma in the Cederberg Mountains and the Victoria and Alfred Waterfront in Cape Town's docklands are but two of many new heritage tourist developments taking place in South Africa that have included black cultures as an important element of their attractions. However, criticism leveled against these projects suggests that while stereotypes may be politically unpalatable, they are of indisputable financial value. Within the tourism industry there is a danger, therefore, of perpetuating the narrow (mis)representations of black cultures in favor of short term gain. Current trends in township tourism suggest that the private sector will not lead this process of transformation in the short term, and that communities themselves lack the skills and finance to support independent ventures. The challenge of transformation has been recognized, but the tourism industry has yet to demonstrate whether it can, indeed, progress beyond apartheid.

Acknowledgments

The authors wish to thank Sue Sayers for her assistance with illustrative material, and Shareen Parker of DATA, for her invaluable comments and input. Richard Young also assisted greatly by providing information related to township tour projects outside Cape Town.

Notes

[1]The Western Cape Province of South Africa (see Map 1) is considered the premiere tourist region of the country, attracting up to 70% of all visitors to South Africa (Cape Metropolitan Council 1994:36).

[2]The word "township" is used to refer to many of South Africa's Black residential areas. These towns were common products of apartheid planning, characterized by inadequate services and poor infrastructure.

[3]The South African unit of currency is the Rand. In June 1996, the Rand/US$ exchange rate was approximately 4.4:1.

[4]The word "Native" was used in the earlier part of this century to refer to South Africans of "African" origin only. This term was one of the earlier apartheid racial classifications and was replaced by the term "Bantu" (see footnote 5).

[5]The word "Bantu" is also a redundant term which referred specifically to indigenous South Africans. The term is no longer in use and is considered derogatory.

[6]According to Rasool and Witz (1994) the term "Bushman," or the Afrikaans equivalent "Bosman," was originally used by Dutch settlers in early colonial times (from the late 1600s to the 1800s) to describe "a heterogeneous collection of people who were dispossessed of their livestock and resisted incorporation in the colonial economy" (ibid.:24). Most of these people were nomadic hunters and gatherers. Today, the term "Bushman," and its alternative "San," are the subject of considerable academic debate regarding their origins and appropriateness as an ethnic label.

[7]Interviews were conducted with ten tour operators who currently undertake tours in Cape Town's Black suburbs. The interviews formed part of a larger community tourism project undertaken by the Environmental and Geographical Science Department at the University of Cape Town.

References

Alexander, P. (1991) "Demolishing the Monument Myth." *Weekly Mail*, 3–9 May.

Beaver, T. (1996) "Kalahari Bushmen on Display at 'Human Zoo'." *Sunday Weekend Argus*, 28 April.

Bickford-Smith, V. and E. Van Heynigen (1994) *The Waterfront*. Cape Town: Oxford University Press.

"Mokaba Taps Into Tourism." (1994) *Business Day* Travel and Tourism Supplement, March 30.

Cape Metropolitan Council (1994) *Tourism Situation Analysis of the Western Cape Region*. Cape Town: Cape Metropolitan Council, Engineering Services.

Central Statistical Services (1994) *South African Labor Statistics*. Pretoria: Central Statistical Services.

Department of Environmental Affairs and Tourism, South Africa (1995) *Tourism Green Paper: Towards a New Tourism Policy for South Africa*. Pretoria: The Interim Tourism Task Team.

Dor, G. (1995) "Tourism and the Community." Paper presented at the Afrotourism '95 Conference, Cape Town 15–16 May.

Douglas, R. (1996) "Bringing Home the Tourists: A New Way to Market Culture." *Weekly Mail and Guardian* Open Africa Supplement, June.

Ecumenical Coalition on Third World Tourism (1995) *Tourism and Indigenous People: A Resource Guide.* Bangkok: Ecumenical Coalition on Third World Tourism.

4U Development Consultants (1995) *Western Cape Tourism Plan and Action Plan: Capacity Building Project For the Western Cape Region.* Unpublished Cape Town Workshop Proceedings Report.

"Gaditshwene." (1993) *Custos* 21(10):18.

Goudie, S. (1993) *Towards a Geography of Leisure: Control, Resistance and Transformation within the South African City.* Unpublished Master's Dissertation, Department of Environmental and Geographical Science, University of Cape Town

"Khaditshwene." (1992) *Custos* 20(2):16.

Khan, F. (1992) "Heritage Conservation: Problems and Proposals," *Conserva* 7(5):8–11

Khan, F. (1993) "Withering Away or Weathering the Twentieth Century?" *Earthyear,* (Spring):26–27.

Kilian, D. (1994) *Change, Conflict and Sense of Place: A Case Study of the Inshore Fishing Community in the Victoria and Alfred Waterfront.* Unpublished Master's Dissertation, Department of Environmental and Geographical Science, University of Cape Town.

Moerdijk, G. (1970) "Design and Symbolism of the Voortrekker Monumnet." In *The Voortrekker Monument, Pretoria—An Official Guide.* Pretoria: Board of Control of the Voortrekker Monument.

Neill, S. (1994) "No Fun for Khoisan Kids." *South* (November):11–15.

Parker, S. (1994) "Case Study: DATA (Development Agency for Tourism Advancement)— Experiences of an Urban CBO." In *Land and Agricultural Policy Center (LAPC) Proceedings (1994): LAPC Tourism Policy Workshop 22–24 November 1994.*

Powell, I. (1994) "Something New, Something Old." *Weekly Mail,* 12–18 August.

Rassool, C. and Witz, L. (1994) "'South Africa: A World in One Country': Moments in International Tourist Encounters with Wildlife, the Primitive and the Modern." Paper Presented at the Center for African Studies, University of Cape Town, September 14.

Richter, L. K. (1995) "Gender and Race: Neglected Variables in Tourism Research." In *Change in Tourism: People, Places, Processes* (edited by Butler, R. and Pearce, D.) London: Routledge.

South African Railways and Harbours (SAR&H) (1935) *The Golden Land: The Sunshine Route—5,000 Miles Through Southern Africa over the South African Railways.* Reprinted in England from the "African" and "Rhodesian" Mining Manuals, Africa House, London.

Tunbridge, J. E. (1984) "Whose Heritage To Conserve? Cross-Cultural Reflections on Political Dominance and Urban Heritage Conservation." *Canadian Geographer* 28(2): 172–180.

Urry, J. (1990) *The Tourist Gaze: Leisure and Travel in Contemporary Societies.* London: Sage Publications.

V&AW Company (1992) "The Essence of the Waterfront." *The Waterfront Review* 1:8–11.

Van Rooyen, G. (1991) *The Waterfront—Cape Town.* Cape Town: Belmore Group.

White, H. (1993) "The Homecoming of the Kagga Kamma Bushmen." In *Cultural Survival Quarterly* (Summer).

Worden, N. (1992) "Unwrapping History at the Cape Town Waterfront." Paper Presented at the History Workshop—Myths, Monuments and Museums, University of the Witwatersrand July 16–18.

Personal Communications:

Bross, R. (1992) Secretary of the Port of Cape Town Fishing Industry Association (POCTFIA), Deep Sea Trawlers Association, and member of the Minister's Liaison Committee, June.

Ozinsky, S. (1992) Education coordinator for the Victoria and Alfred Waterfront Company, August.

Parker, S. (1996) Founder of Development Agency for Tourism Advancement (DATA), April / May 1996.

Representative of the Planning Department of the Cape Town City Council (1996), May.

5

PUSHED TO THE LIMITS—THE DYNAMICS OF INTERNAL NEO-COLONIALISM IN PERIPHERAL TOURISM DEVELOPMENTS: CASE STUDIES IN EGYPT AND SOUTH WALES

JOSEY PETFORD

One of the primary objects of colonialism is to add to the productive base of a nation state through the annexation of another country's resources, to add to reserves of raw materials and to create new markets to which the home country can then sell its products. The cultural effects of colonialism can vary from the attempted total annihilation of peoples and cultures, as practised by the European nations colonizing North America in the Age of Expansion, to the exploitation of native cultures for the benefit of the colonizers, as happened more recently under British colonial rule in India. However, the main driving force of colonialism has always been economic and the pressure to exploit any available resource is no less now than it has ever been. Under neo-colonialism the resources in most demand from the Third World are cheap labor, agricultural land and unspoilt wilderness, all resources which the First World feels it no longer possesses in sufficient quantities to meet the increasing demands of its populations and industries.

Culturally the Third World is also subject to the demands of the First World. Increasingly the religions, art, clothing, food and architecture of the Third World (Root 1996) are becoming commodities to be exploited for the fashions of the First, further threatening life ways which are already stressed by the encroaching global economy. The connection between these two levels of exploitation, the cultural and the economic, I would argue, is to a large extent negotiated through the tourist experience. Many tourists travelling to Third World, or Less Developed, countries will be encouraged to view the vernacular life of the natives, sample local food, purchase goods from the local market as souvenirs. On their return to their home country they may well find those self-same goods in their local stores. Businesses such as Body Shop increasingly exploit the opening of the Third World to tourism in their marketing strategies, building on the burgeoning base of familiar yet commercially exotic images of Rousseauesque vernacular life.

It has been argued (Root 1996) that in a post-Fordist, niche marketing economy there is no limit to what consumers can buy and that, in our postmodern world, there is no sector of the economy that can avoid plundering the cultures of others to meet the demands of fashion and consumer choice. The holiday business is no exception, as yesterday's exotic locations rapidly become destinations for the two-week family vacation. In this increasingly competitive world the need to find new attractions to entice the fickle tourist away from the competition and into your own resort is of paramount importance, potentially relegating concerns about possible environmental and cultural impacts to a poor second in the face of the commercial imperative to remain viable and increase visitor numbers. One result of this trend is that areas, such as historic Eastern Europe or inner city industrial sites, which were not previously considered as mass tourist destinations, are being earmarked for development, particularly where a brand new attraction can be discovered or manufactured to add an element of originality to the holiday. In this paper I will consider the implications of this trend for two areas: South Wales in Britain, where I have lived for six years and studied its growing market in cultural tourism, and Siwa, a Berber oasis in the Western Desert which is the current and future location of my fieldwork.

Theoretical Background

Ernest Gellner speaks about the geographical distribution of Berber societies in North Africa in his analysis of the role of religious leaders in segmentary societies, *Saints of the Atlas*, saying

> This pattern resembles that of Celtic-speaking territory in Britain: a set of discontinuous pockets, some large, some small ... The reason for this discontinuity and occupancy of backwoods terrain is the same in both cases. Berbers are the survivors of the earlier inhabitants of North Africa, displaced in the richer plains and the towns by the later comers, and surviving in less accessible regions (Gellner 1969:13).

In this paper I will take Gellner's idea further, highlighting the similarities between the position of Siwa vis à vis national government and international business, and that of Wales, one of the British regions which claims a Celtic identity. I will argue that although tourism may not be the only cause of internal neo-colonialism, it does, in these cases, build on existing economic and social structures in order to more fully exploit all elements of the cultures and that within that exploitation lies the perpetuation of colonial attitudes and relationships.

Anthropological definitions of neo-colonialism allow us to look more closely at the internal neocolonialism (de Kadt 1979:24) found in Siwa and Wales as they recognize "the creation of an elite within the colonized nation which will perpetuate relations of dependency..." (Seymour-Smith 1986:207) alongside the dynamics of structural and economic domination. The position of this elite within such countries today, particularly those with a cultural or ethnic minority, result in internal neo-colonialism, whereby the culture and resources of a relatively powerless minority are exploited by the elite or majority with little or no consultation with the exponents and traditional owners. Weedon and Jordan offer the following working analysis of the features of the colonial relationship, "The power to name. The power to represent common sense. The power to create official versions. The power to represent the legitimate social world" (Jordan and Weedon 1995:13).

The product which tourism offers the consumer differs significantly from other products' in distinctive ways as the product must be consumed in situ rather than in the comfort of the consumer's own home (Lea 1988), and also because, what is sold is a dream or an image, rather than a concrete artifact (Selwyn 1995). Hence definitions of neo-colonialism which rely on economic, political or cultural grounds individually, cannot describe the experience of internal neo-colonialism in the tourist destination. However, if Jordan and Weedon's definition, which has its roots in cultural studies, is combined with the anthropological, including the concept of elites with economic and political domination, we start to approach a working definition of neo-colonialism which, by encompassing economic, political and cultural elements, can be applied to tourism.

The Case Studies: Siwa Oasis, Egypt, and South Wales, Britain

Despite their superficial disparity, the histories of the two areas show certain interesting parallels, despite the fact that Wales has been under English rule for approximately 1000 years, a situation formalized in the Act of Union, 1536 (Thomas 1991:45) and Siwa, although being technically part of Egypt for many centuries, has until recently remained relatively autonomous and immune from central government control. As Gellner (1969) predicts, geographically both Siwa and Wales constitute areas that are remote from political and economic centers and are populated by a minority people. This is evidenced through language use with Welsh, rather than English, historically, being the first language of Wales, and Berber still being spoken in Siwa alongside Egyptian Arabic. They have had their own political and religious traditions distinct from those of the nation within which they are situated and rich oral histories evidenced through both folklore and music.

Background Information: Siwa

Siwa lies just 15 km from the Libyan border, a factor which makes the town an area of military significance for Egypt. The only road access to the oasis is via the desert road which follows Masrab al-Istabl, the old caravan route, from

Marsa Matruh 300km away on the coast. Public transport is regular, consisting of two buses per day, but of variable quality as the vehicles themselves are extremely rough and ready. Currently Siwa entertains approximately 1,000 tourists per year, who fall primarily into the category of backpackers or other independent travellers. Consequently, all tourists have to get military clearance in order to travel to Siwa, and this intrepid band have to contend with more than the typical travel restrictions. Hotel accommodation varies in quality from passable to very poor, and is mainly situated in the town centre. Other accomodation includes an area which is used by backpackers for camping, although it has none of the expected facilities provided which could allow it to be described as a campsite, e.g. water or sewage. The Berber population, who number about 10,000, rely predominantly on their gardens for subsistence, still growing the dates and olives which they have exported to the coast and the major cities for hundreds of years. However, all this is about to change, as the oasis has been selected by the Egyptian government for tourist development on a scale comparative to that in Upper Egypt.

New Attractions

About three miles outside Siwa town in an area called Marakia, there is a current archeological dig partly funded by the Egyptian government and supervised by Greek archeologist Liana Soulvatsis. On this site she claims to have discovered the much sought after burial site of Alexander the Great, a goal that has eluded archeologists, and other seekers, for hundreds of years. This discovery, although strongly contested and as yet unproven, is not implausible. Alexander's body disappeared after it was stolen by Ptolemy, Alexander's successor in Egypt, and there is evidence in the written record that Alexander requested that he be buried at the Oasis of the Oracle. Twelve years before his death, at the beginning of his meteoric rise to world power, Alexander had visited the Oracle of Amun and, although he never revealed what he had asked of the god, this visit evidently had a profound influenced on his life because ever after he demonstrated a personal devotion to Zeus Amun. Apparently the oracle had given Alexander confirmation of his divine nature as a son of Amun and the rise of Alexander was reflected in the increased kudos accruing to the Siwan oracle (Lane Fox 1993). The academic authentication of the site is, in some ways, irrelevant to the government, although it would lend added weight to arguments in favor of developing the area. Currently the Egyptian government is quite willing to sell land in the area, trading on the possibility that the site may be genuine, while concurrently preparing to implement a rapid development policy in the event that Alexander's tomb is authenticated. Siwa is an important army base monitoring Egypt's border with Libya and the movements of Bedouin who still act as couriers across that part of the desert. The base has a small military airport which the government claims it can transform into a civil one overnight to allow visitors to avoid the long and arduous journey from Marsah Matruh. The authentication of the Alexander's tomb site could leave the small population of Marakia facing a difficult future. It has been suggested that it would be impossible for them to continue to live on the site, meaning that they would have to abandon their gardens and move back into the main town where fertile land and building plots are scarce. However, the population of the town itself is also under threat of relocation and I was told that the people would obey if the order came from central government for them to move out.

Environmental Impact

There are also serious environmental implications inherant in any tourism development at Siwa which are currently attracting little attention from either international agencies or from the Egyptian government. The main archeological attractions of Siwa are the remains of the Temple of the Oracle of Amun; the Hill of the Dead, Jabal al-Mawta, situated about a mile outside the town and containing exquisite examples of Greco-Egyptian wall painting; and the remaining wall of the Temple of Umm Ubaydah. This latter site probably exemplifies the environmental problems more than any other. The temple of Umm Ubaydah had survived relatively intact until it was blown up in 1897 by a Ma'mur (Shayk) who wanted to use the stones for the staircase of his new residence and to construct a new police station (Fakhry 1973:165). Beside the surviving wall there lie a number of fallen stones which, at first sight, seem to be undecorated. However a closer look at other stones whose surfaces lie facing the ground show that the remains were actually covered in carvings which have been obliterated by decades of graffiti.

The vernacular architecture of the town was, traditionally, built using a combination of salt and sand and the houses constructed in layers giving the old town an organic look somewhat reminiscent of a termite mound. Although this technique and these materials are proof against most weather, even the occasional shower which the oasis receives, it cannot stand against torrential rain and floods such as those which occured in 1984 when about half the people lost their homes. Traditional materials have been abandoned during rebuilding and today the majority of the population live in single story houses built from breeze block, a design which allows services (electricity, plumbing and telephone) to be installed more easily. The population appears to be divided along gender lines on the benefits of this change with the men considering the move detrimental to family life while the women preferring the new houses which can accommodate televisions and washing machines.

Currently there is little or no supervision at most of the sites and the high exposed old town and Temple of the Oracle are potentially lethal to unwary sightseers with their sharp unprotected and unmarked drops and steep footpaths. How, or even if, these sites could be protected from further deterioration and damage by the weather and human incursion without changing their naive vernacular nature which constitutes a major part of their value to the average tourist, is problematic. Paradoxically one proposed hotel development is to take the form of a replica of the old town which is to be built on the top of a nearby mountain. A fine sense of irony is required to appreciate the prospect of the Siwan population watching their old town destroyed by the very feet which will simultaneously be residing in the town's more robustly built and well equipped simulacrum.

Although Siwa is well serviced with electricity and telephone lines it has no mains sewage provision. Traditionally this presented no problems for the Siwans as they used their waste to fertilize their gardens. However the oasis has a severe problem with standing water which is interfering with the traditional method of sewage disposal as many of the areas where waste was spread out to dry in the sun are now under water. This problem will only be exacerbated by an increase in tourist numbers unless some other method of sewage treatment is found. Current proposals are for the untreated sewage to be buried in the desert a solution which, although quite feasible if the site remains small, could potentially lead to a serious pollution problem if growth is vast and uncontrolled

Background Information: South Wales

South Wales is a longstanding holiday destination for travellers in Britain. It offers sun, sea and sand holidays on the beaches of Pembrokeshire and the Gower peninsula, and walking holidays across the Black Mountains and in the South Wales valleys. It is well supplied with hotels, bed and breakfast, farmhouse and self-catering cottage accommodation. Access to some sites and resorts is a major problem, particularly in southwest Wales, which is not serviced by the national motorway network which relieves the pressure on the main A road system in other areas. This can result in severe traffic hold-ups on bank holidays and during the holiday season, and represents a major barrier to commercial investment in southwest Wales. Some attempt has been made to remedy this but currently funding is not available to extend the M4 motorway past Swansea. Tourism has, however, always been of secondary importance to the people of south Wales as a source of income as they have historically subsisted through dairy and sheep farming and working in the iron and coal industries. In recent years this pattern has changed. With new European community (EC) rules on milk quotas reducing available income from dairy farming increasing numbers of farmers have refurbished their farm buildings, turning them into holiday cottages that can be let out to tourists. Industrial workers can no longer find employment in their traditional industries. The iron and steel industry has all but collapsed and the only working coal mine the whole of South Wales is now privately owned by its workforce, having been sold off by the British Coal as it pulled out of the South Wales coalfield in the late 1980s.

New Attractions

Many of the old industrial sites are now being converted into heritage parks in an attempt to attract the cultural tourist to South Wales. Such working sites as Big Pit and the Rhondda Heritage Park offer the tourist the chance to experience life as a miner with guided tours around the workings complete with authentic sights, sounds and smells. There have also been recent initiatives to change the way in which Welsh history is presented in the National Museum of Wales, both at its site in St Fagan's where the National Welsh Folk Museum has metamorphisized into the Museum of Welsh Life and in Cardiff, which have historically been centers of research into Welsh history and lifeways. As funding from central government is cut the new emphasis is on visitor numbers and so the focus has moved onto the visitor experience rather than academic excellence.

Environmental Problems

The majority of environmental problems suffered by South Wales are those commonly experienced by heavily developed First World regions. An increasing number of vehicles on the roads leads not only to traffic jams but also to high levels of exhaust gases around major routes. There also problems with water supplies and with sewage treatment; however, none of these are particularly influenced by tourists. Rather, in South Wales it is environmental problems which have had an effect on tourists, in particular the recent major oil spill off the Pembrokeshire coast which polluted many beaches and destroyed the wildlife which was one of the area's major tourist attractions. At first it appeared that visitor numbers would be radically reduced; however, this has not proved to be as serious as was first feared although bookings were down about 15% on previous years. The long-term effects of the disaster could be more severe because, even though the clean-up operation has been partially successful, Pembroke's beaches no longer fly the EC blue flag which proves them to be clean, safe beaches, and at times visitors are prevented from swimming due to the high levels of pollutant in the water.

Economic Relationships

It is equally clear that on an economic level the relationship between the people, local elites, central government and international corporations is similar in Britain and Egypt. After years of perceived English exploitation of their coal, iron and slate deposits, the Welsh people have few material resources left and the closure of mines and steelworks in the last forty years has left nearly all areas of Wales suffering from high levels of poverty and unemployment. To counteract this decline Wales is trying to attract new industries to its more deprived areas; however, the majority of the funding for developments, taking the form of grants or favorable tax breaks, comes from either central government or, increasingly, from private business rather than from locally accountable sources. One example, among many, of this tendency is the Cardiff Bay Development Corporation (which, it is hoped, will become the central feature of a new and lucrative tourism industry based on the business and conference tourist) and in particular the Pengam Green development consisting of housing, industrial and leisure facilities. The main funding for this scheme comes from the French investor Credit Agricole, with the remainder coming from central government (Cardiff Bay Development Corporation n.d.:6.) As the corporation is operating a free market policy, it may be presumed that the majority of the profits from this venture will be relocated to France or back to the British government.

The role of international business in Siwa is, currently, somewhat smaller; however, the only large factory in the town, a water bottling plant, is owned and run by an Italian firm (which has also recently purchased a piece of land on which to build a large hotel complex). Water is one of the few raw materials which Siwa possesses in any quantity, and an agreement was reached between the local council and the bottling firm which guaranteed that 0.01 piastres would be paid to local people per litre of water bottled. This agreement is not currently being fulfilled, and the central government is doing nothing to remedy the situation, which is unsurprising as foreign investment of this type is such an important priority for the Egyptian government. Another example of the attractive terms and conditions available to the foreign investor can be found in the Tourist Development Authority brochure:

> The right of profit repatriation and re-exportation of invested funds, tax exemptions ranging up to 10 years, custom duty on imported equipment and machinery at 5% flat rate, elimination of controls on prices and profit ceilings, and right of acquisition of land and real estate (Tourism Development Authority n.d.).

The results of this policy would, it could be predicted, be an almost total leakage of profit and investment from Egypt to the country of investment. The infrastructure which results from a high level of foreign investment would not be owned by the Egyptians and will predominantly be out of their control. The Siwan people will be at an even greater disadvantage, not even having the small amount of control which central government retains. The situation is further complicated in Siwa by their system of recording land ownership and registration. The traditional system of recording all transactions in a book owned by the family is not recognized by the Egyptian government and currently a two-tier system is in operation whereby incoming investors purchase land in the first instance from the government and only subsequently from its Siwan owners. On a national level, the Egyptian government considers Siwa a priority area for tourist development, and under the agreement reached during the Uruguay round of the GATT talks it is prevented from instituting restrictive barriers against the purchase of land by foreign nationals. Excluding the government-owned hotel, all the others in the town are owned and run by Egyptians as opposed to Siwans, and there is a high a level of apathy from some sectors of the population towards becoming involved in the tourist business at all. Although this level of leakage from the economic periphery to center is symptomatic of many economic transactions, it is typically considered in the context of the exploitation of Third World countries by the First World, rather than through internal neo-colonialism within the First or Third World.

There seems little doubt that the amount of control over the economy by external investors and the local elite in both Siwa and Wales constitutes internal neo-colonialism in an economic context; however, as discussed above, any definition which is to be applicable to tourism also demands that this exists on the political and cultural levels, which are, in any case, inseparably linked to economic factors.

Political Relationships

The level of political alienation in Siwa is already severe for, although there is a local council to handle the day-to-day running of the town which consists of representatives of each of the local families appointed by the shayks, the area comes under the jurisdiction of the Governor of the Masa Matruh area. Such regional governors are Egyptians from influential families appointed by central government (often retired politicians or army officers) who do not necessarily have any personal commitment to, or knowledge of, the area. All major decisions, anything beyond the routine running of the town, such as road building or infrastructure improvements, have to be referred through his office. The results of this are graphically illustrated by the government decision to undertake a major road building project in the area which cost approximately £E 24 million and cut only four miles from the relatively unused existing route. In contrast to this investment, the Siwan council has been unsuccessfully requesting financial help from central government, totalling around £E 2 million, for about ten years, to help alleviate the severe water drainage problem on the oasis.

This lack of communication, whether deliberate or accidental, contributes to increasing feelings of alienation from the political system among local people. Egypt is ostensibly a democratic system yet the Siwans have no voice in decisions which effect their community. It might be expected that peripheral peoples would fare better under the Mother of Parliaments; however, this is not the case for the Welsh. Politically Wales is governed by the English Parliament through the Welsh Office, and in economical development by a QUANGO (Quasi-autonomous non-governmental organization) known as the Welsh Development Agency, under the direct control of the Welsh Office (WDA 1978).

Although Wales elects its own local government representatives, their powers
are severely restricted and the majority of decisions which involve government
capital investment are out of local control, and lie in the hands of the Welsh
Office and through them with Whitehall and central government (Betts 1996).

Again, the Cardiff Bay development is a prime example of a centralized
decision making process overriding the needs and wants of the local population. The area which has been developed is an area primarily inhabited by Cardiff's longstanding immigrant population. It was perceived as being poverty
stricken and culturally stagnant; hence it was decided, by private investors and
the Welsh Development Agency, that the area was a prime site for industrial and
cultural redevelopment. Much of the indigenous population, both residential
and industrial, were relocated (Thomas et al. 1989) and the existing buildings
replaced with privately owned apartments and business units, not unlike those
found in London Docklands (Cardiff Bay Development Corporation 1988:26)
but unaffordable to most of the previous inhabitants.

Cultural Relationships

Intrinsically tied to weak political representation is a lack of power to represent
cultural norms and to control the image used to market an area. The domination
of Wales by English colonists has led to a skewed representation of Welsh history, turning South Wales into the chapel-going, rugby-playing miners with
whom most tourists are familiar from brochures for the Land of Song (Geraint
Jenkins 1992). External control over capital investment has meant that it is very
difficult for those images that do not which fit the English conception of
Welshness, and developments which use or distribute such images, to gain substantial investment (Jordan and Weedon 1995). The culture of the Cardiff dockland area, a complex admixture reflecting successive waves of immigration
and consisting of, among others, Irish, Yemeni, West Indian and Chinese elements, was largely disregarded by the Cardiff Bay Development Corporation
(CBDC), and, when a museum was included in the redevelopment plans, local
people have had to fight to have the diversity of their culture adequately represented, primarily through the Butetown History & Arts Project (Jordan and
Weedon 1995:112–73). As Tiger Bay represents one of the major features of
Cardiff in popular culture this marginalization of its people by the CBDC seems
indicative of an attempt to sanitize and depoliticize an area and a population
which was in the forefront of Britain's attempts to come to terms with her multi-
cultural post-colonial position and to marginalize an area with a high political
profile.

In Siwa, cultural internal colonialism currently appears to have little impact
as the area and its culture has been regarded as having little value by the Egyptian authorities. They have established, with the help of a Canadian Aid Agency
a museum of traditional Siwan life called The House of Siwa. However, despite

the fact that the museum quite adequately illustrates some of the clothing and jewelry of the oasis and explains some of the history of the town, it concentrates almost exclusively on female culture and the culture of the home. If tourist numbers increase it is the men's culture that will be under threat, their stories, songs, cultivation techniques and social life which will be lost as the young men leave the land to take work in the hotels.

Additionally, if future tourist developments are considered in the light of events in the rest of Egypt there is the possibility of antipathy developing between Siwans and visitors. There is some level of stress already evident, and worries have been expressed that the culture of Siwa is under threat from both secular Muslim and non-Muslim tourists who do not respect local custom. For example, gender segregation in Siwa is very strict with adult women always appearing completely veiled when in public, and no intoxicating liquor (excepting the local brew *labgi*, fermented palm heart, which is occasionally given as a gift within private homes) is available anywhere on the oasis. Currently tourists are requested, via a notice on the map of Siwa available from the Tourism Office, not to drink alcohol (which they are allowed to bring with them) in public and for women to keep their arms and legs covered, controls which are aimed at protecting the culture of the host population from the impact which contact with tourists can have. The enforcement of this request, however, seems to be potentially problematic to the Siwans and when asked what law could be used to enforce the request, the Tourism Officer did not appear to believe that anyone would be rude enough to disobey.

If the rest of Egypt is taken as an example of tourist behavior patterns it is unlikely that these rules will be enforced by incoming businesses or practiced by the majority of visitors. The results could well be an upsurge of Islamic fundamentalism and anti-Westerner feeling not unlike that already occurring in Upper and Middle Egypt, which would lead to increased political alienation between Muslim Siwans and the secular Egyptian government. Indeed there is already a small fundamentalist movement whose main criticism is levelled at female visitors who do not cover themselves properly and an underlying belief developing that tourists, like television, have a detrimental influence on traditional morals and values.

Gender Relations

Against this background of political and cultural relations, both Siwa and Wales are undergoing profound cultural and economic changes in gender dynamics. The economy of Siwa is male dominated with, superficially at least, men appearing to hold sway in the political and economic arena; however, women are perceived as the bearers of tradition, responsible for passing on the culture and language of Siwa to the next generation. The men, particularly the younger men, wear clothes in an Egyptian or European style, and mix freely with both male and female tourists, and are able to pursue their schooling to a higher level in Alexandria or Cairo, unlike the majority of girls who leave school at puberty. Gender segregation is strictly enforced in Siwa, all adult women wrap themselves in a *milayah*, a large black and grey striped cloth, when they have to leave the house. When inside their homes, however, the women wear beautifully embroidered colorful shawls, blouses and trousers and these items have proved popular among tourists with many being sold on the streets in Siwa or sent for sale in Cairo. Traditionally women were excluded from the means of production because, although women were allowed to own land, they were forbidden from working in the gardens, thus having to rely on the men in their family to make the land productive. However, the sale of handicrafts has led to a situation not previously experienced in Siwa before, where women have access to a fairly large and independent source of cash income which could easily exceed that of the men.

Although there is nothing like the level of gender segregation in Wales it has, traditionally, also been very male dominated economically and politically, and until recently, men and women even socialized separately. However, this pattern of increasing reliance on female wages rather than a male family wage is also common to Wales, where "Mam," the traditional bearer of culture and the person in charge of domestic matters within the home, has moved out into the workplace to provide the family with an income (Aaron et al. 1994). It is projected that between 1994 and 2006 the female workforce in Wales will have increased by 9.5%, whereas that for men will have grown by only 0.8% (Welsh Office 1995) and present patterns suggest that they will also continue in their primary role as mothers and homekeepers, leaving Welsh men in the ambiguous position of being neither breadwinner nor primary carer.

The long-term effects of these changes in Siwa and South Wales are not identifiable, however whether they prove to be positive or negative for women and their families or the communities in which they live, they will do little in the short term to change the structure of their societies. It is unlikely that any of the Siwan women or their children will rise to the rank of Governor or President, revolutionize the political system and give the Siwans a voice; it is equally unlikely that they will suddenly find themselves in a position to compete with international business on an economic level. Likewise women in Wales have to find some way of breaking through the glass ceiling, described by Teresa Rees as "double-glazed" in recognition of its particularly robust nature in Wales (Rees 1994:96).

Conclusions

Within Britain and Egypt there exist relationships of internal neo-colonialism between the center and periphery based on a local elite which retains political control over the peripheral regions, and which removes important decision making powers from local people and into the hands of that elite. Culturally, that elite has the power to name, to represent common sense, to create official versions, and to represent the legitimate social world. In both Siwa and South Wales these powers are implemented through national tourism policies, the decisions about how and where to invest, and which cultural norms to support and present to visitors and, economically the two regions are regarded as sources of income for international business, central government and the local/national elite.

When looking at any tourist market, whether based on the development of a new site or changes to an existing one, it is vital to look at the context of that development, at existing and residual social, political and economic relationships, as within those relationships lie not only the clues to many of the major barriers afflicting the development of an ethical and sustainable tourism industry but also the seeds of how to make any such development successful.

I have tried to show in this paper how those structures and relationships can, through internal neo-colonialism, allow the imposition of cultural and economic programmes for tourism in peripheral areas who lack the political and economic power to control the development. This is by no means the whole story. Wales is slowly reclaiming its own heritage, and, on the margins of the tourist industry, is carving a new, less stereotypical, image for itself. If the projected Welsh assembly becomes a reality it could offer the opportunity for Wales to regain a level of self-government, or at least have a greater voice in the running of its own affairs. But much of the progress made in Wales is due to a long history of rebellion against authority and a tradition of radical politics. There is no such history in Siwa and the Siwan people, as only one minority people in a country which boasts several, have little chance to have their voice heard outside their own oasis. However, the projected developments have not yet taken place and so there is still time to offer them a voice, to try to convince the Egyptian government that Siwan culture and way of life are worth protecting, not simply as a tourist attraction but because it, and the people themselves, have a value in their own right.

References

Aaron, J., T. Rees, S. Betts and M. Vincentelli, eds. (1994) *Our Sisters' Land: The Changing Identities of Women in Wales*. Cardiff: University of Wales Press.

Betts, C. (1996) "Welsh Office powerless to fight for Wales." *The Western Mail*, 23 May, 1.

Cardiff Bay Development Corporation (n.d.) *Cardiff Bay—The Opportunity*. Promotional Material. Cardiff: Cardiff Bay Development Corporation.

Cardiff Bay Development Corporation (1988) *Cardiff Bay Regeneration Strategy*. Cardiff: Cardiff Bay Development Corporation.

De Kadt, E., ed. (1979) *Tourism, Passport to Development?: Perspectives on the So-*

cial and Cultural Effects of Tourism in Developing Countries. Oxford: Oxford University Press.

Fakhry, A. (1973) The Oases of Egypt. Vol. 1. Siwa Oasis. Cairo: American University in Cairo Press.

Gellner, E. (1969) Saints of the Atlas. London: Weidenfield and Nicholson.

Geraint Jenkins, J. (1992) Getting Yesterday Right: Interpreting the Heritage of Wales. Cardiff: University of Wales Press.

Jordan, G. and Weedon, C. (1995) Cultural Politics: Class, Gender, Race and the Postmodern World. Oxford: Blackwell.

Lane Fox, R. (1973) Alexander the Great. London: Penguin.

Lea, J. (1988) Tourism and Development in the Third World. London: Routledge.

Rees, T. (1994) "Women and paid work in Wales." In Our Sisters' Land: The Changing Identities of Women in Wales (edited by Aaron, J. et al.) Cardiff: University of Wales Press.

Root, D. (1996) Cannibal Culture: Art, Appropriation and the Commodification of Difference. Oxford: Westview Press.

Selwyn, T., ed. (1996) The Tourist Image: Myths and Mythmaking in Tourism. London: John Wiley and Sons Ltd.

Seymour-Smith, C. (1986) Macmillan Dictionary of Anthropology. London: Macmillan.

Thomas, H. (1991) A History of Wales, 1485–1660. Cardiff: University of Wales Press.

Thomas, H., R. Imrie and P. Griffiths (1989) "An Extravagant Nonsense?" The Effects of a Compulsory Purchase Order on Firms in Cardiff Docklands. Cardiff: Regional Industrial Research.

Tourism Development Authority (n.d.) Tourism Development Authority: Designated Tourism Areas. Cairo: TDA.

Welsh Development Agency (1978) The Strategy of the Welsh Development Agency for the Provision of Finance and Advice to Industry in Wales. Pontypridd: Welsh Development Agency.

Welsh Office (1995) Welsh Economic Trends (Tueddiadau'r Economi) No. 16. Government Statistical Office.

6

Cultural Tourism in Appalachian Tennessee

Jean Haskell Speer

The Appalachian Mountain Region extends along the entire mountain range of the eastern United States. However, in the popular mind, Appalachia means the southern part of the mountains, from West Virginia to north Georgia, and including the mountainous portions of Tennessee. The southern highlands have long been a tourist destination in the United States, both for their natural beauty and the cultural attractions of the region. Promotion of culture in the region has centered on those features typical of most mountain areas—isolation, primitiveness, innocence, ruggedness, quaintness—in short, all those characteristics antithetical and desirable to the "over-civilized."

Important issues emerge from critical study of the history of tourism in the Appalachian mountains and examination of cultural tourism in Appalachia today. These issues include the shaping of cultural identity, cultural hegemony, the relationship of culture to economic and public policy in the region, and shifting conceptions of culture. This study examines three significant periods of tourism development in Appalachia, the current status of tourism in the region, and possible scenarios for future development of tourism in the region.

From Eden to Evolution

Appalachia was first inhabited by Native Americans who hunted and farmed the mountains long before any Europeans saw the region. The Indians, primarily Cherokee in Tennessee and North Carolina, lived according to a harmony ethic, keeping the natural and human world in balance through ritual and restraint. In 1540, the region was explored and named by the Hernando DeSoto expedition, looking for gold to extract from the region; by 1562, the name "Appalachen" appears on European maps. The name, derived from an Indian tribe, connoted "place of gold" to the Europeans.

The identification of the mountain region soon led explorers to map it and seek out its riches. The earliest explorers called the region a "paradise, an Eden" for its unspoiled beauty and richness. By the end of the seventeenth century, the region was becoming settled by European immigrants looking for land and freedom of lifestyle. The southern Appalachians were first a homeland, but with inherent attractions that would soon make them a tourist destination. By the middle of the nineteenth century, Appalachia's mountains, like the mountains of Europe, were garnering the attention of nostalgic tourists and industrial developers alike.

Railroads were built throughout the mountains shortly after the Civil War to develop the region's rich natural resources—timber, coal and other minerals, and water—to support burgeoning industries such as steel production in the northeast and textiles in the south. Railroads built to industrialize the previously undeveloped region also brought the first significant tourist penetration of Appalachia, including pilgrims to mountain healing springs and spas, local color writers, photographers, and early silent film makers. These tourists brought changes in land use and land values to the region and began to establish the parameters of Appalachian culture in American consciousness. Wealthy summer tourists began to buy land and build summer homes in the cool and disease-free mountains. The Vanderbilts, for example, built a fabulous French chateau on thousands of acres near Asheville, North Carolina. Land values began to soar in areas that attracted these wealthy non-natives.

As changes in the land occurred, so did perceptions of local culture. The summer tourists, wealthy and cosmopolitan, found the indigenous residents of the region at best "quaint" and at worst "primitive and uncivilized." These attitudes about people in the mountains were communicated to the world beyond the mountains by writers who described local color in ways that created a mythology of Appalachian life based on otherness, primitiveness, and ignorance. One writer described the mountain region as "a strange land with peculiar people" (Harney 1873). Perceptions of early tourists in Appalachia paralleled similar nineteenth-century attitudes in Europe toward mountain areas: ambivalences resulting from positive feelings about the natural environment of the mountains and uncertain or negative feelings about mountain people. In Europe, this was a period that celebrated the beauty of the mountains through Romantic poets, admired the legendary story of freedom fighter William Tell, and lamented, as French writer Elisée Reclus did, the goitered, mountain cretins who looked and acted like savages or "monsters" (Reclus 1881). So entrenched were these attitudes that one American writer of the period created a story of a half-wild, but charming and graceful Appalachian girl that he christened "a mountain Europa" (Fox 1909).

These perceptions of mountain people in the late nineteenth and early twentieth centuries reflected prevailing theories of culture based on cultural evolutionism and cultural survivals. Cultural evolution held that societies were constantly evolving toward higher levels of "civilization" (defined by social, technological, and financial complexity), so that cultures could be classified roughly as savage, adolescent, or mature. Cultural survivals (e.g. vestiges of English ballad singing in Appalachia) indicated the culture was still in an earlier stage than a mature, industrial society. Appalachia, and indeed most mountain societies, were thought at the time to be adolescent; primitive but with potential.

This view had two major effects: waves of educators, clergy, and social reformers poured into the mountains to help the "poor mountaineers" move toward the next level of civilization and those elements of mountain life that seemed to be remnants of an earlier, simpler time came to be highly valued and catapulted into significance beyond their importance in local culture.

Tourism, which had become an important part of the mountain economy, drew on the cultural survivals or "folk" elements of the culture to entice travelers. Appalachia became a place to see simple folk making baskets, weaving coverlets, quilting, playing banjos and singing old ballads in a pristine mountain land. These motifs became the focus for travel brochures, travel writing and illustrations, and photographs. What this static image of Appalachia masked was a revolution taking place in a culture torn asunder by industrialization (timbering, coal mining, etc.), growing urbanization, and mass commercialism. But this period set the stage for future developments in tourism in the region.

From Stereotype to Strategic Planning

The second significant period of tourism came at the close of World War II, when Americans enjoyed new prosperity and leisure time. The purchase of family automobiles and changes in work patterns made "vacations" available to most Americans for the first time. Driving to the mountains and to the new national parks that had been created in the 1930s and 1940s became a national trend. Services for tourists—motels, restaurants, and souvenir shops—mushroomed. The motels, restaurants, and souvenirs often used popular perceptions of the region for their appeal. These popular perceptions in the mid-twentieth century centered either on the romantic notions of the noble, independent mountaineer, created in the previous century and echoing William Tell, or the caricatures of the lazy, gun-toting, moonshine-drinking, poor and stupid hillbilly that had emerged from mass media (cartoons such as *L'il Abner* about a fictional hillbilly community were widely known to the public).

The national parks in the Appalachian region, the Shenandoah National Park, the Great Smoky Mountains National Park, and the Blue Ridge Parkway, developed and promoted cultural resources as well as natural resources. Drawing on the tradition of earlier tourism efforts, national park policy in the region focused on preservation of the "pioneer culture" of Appalachia to the exclusion of all other cultural dynamics. Cultural planning for tourists centered on vernacular architecture, traditional crafts and music, and regional customs; however, cultural patterns that did not fit the park model of the pioneer past were ignored or even delegitimized through legislation.

An interesting example of this cultural tunnel vision occurred along the Blue Ridge Parkway in the mountain section of Virginia. A small, yet thriving community in the mountains, called Mons, was lost to the demands of this pioneer culture plan for tourism in the national park. Mons had developed from a tiny settlement, established in the late eighteenth century, at the base of two scenic mountain peaks (a settlement ironically originating from a tourist hostel). Located on a turnpike and attractive to tourists, Mons soon became a thriving community; by the early twentieth century it consisted of a large tourist hotel, twenty family homes and farms, public buildings such as a school and meeting hall, and an economy based on agriculture, including the export of large apple crops to England, and tourism. In the 1930s, when the United States government decided to create a scenic roadway, the Blue Ridge Parkway, through the area, the land was purchased, the Victorian hotel torn down, and community virtually obliterated. In its place, a lake and a new tourist lodge were built. The only part of the Mons community that survived was a small mountain farm that could be made to fit the pioneer culture profile.[1] A similar experience occurred in the Cades Cove section of Tennessee that is now part of the Great Smoky Mountains National Park, a story well-documented in Durwood Dunn's *Cades Cove: The Life and Death of a Southern Appalachian Community, 1818–1937* (Dunn 1988).

Even as the parks continued to present the long-held view of Appalachia as a static culture, the onslaught of tourism brought to the region in part by the parks was causing dramatic changes. Growth around the peripheries of the parks exploded with little planning or control. What had been small, sleepy mountain villages became villages choked with traffic and tourists; environmental pollution increased with more and more car emissions, solid waste, and noise; visual blight in the form of signs, billboards, and glitzy, trashy tourist attractions blocked out mountain views. And local culture often lost its integrity in a rush to pander to tourist expectations. For example, some mountain residents "became" the hillbillies the tourists were hoping to see, wearing costume and over-playing mountain dialect in their speech. Native Cherokee Indians dressed up in head-dresses and set up roadside teepees for tourists to photograph; the Cherokees had never worn head-dresses (these were common to western Plains Indians) nor lived in teepees, but this was what the tourists expected of Indians.

These effects of too much tourism, coupled with growing awareness of ecological concerns and heightened sensitivity to the cultural identity of the region, marked a shift in cultural tourism efforts in Appalachia in the late 1970s and 1980s. In efforts to reclaim the cultural integrity of Appalachia and promote cultural pluralism in the region, museums and other tourist attractions based on more accurate portrayals of mountain life sprang up throughout the mountains. For example, the Museum of the Cherokee Indian presents accurate views of Cherokee myth and ritual, lifestyle, and cultural contributions to counteract the head-dressed, teepeed stereotypes tourists still can see. A museum of Appalachian culture in one mountain town shows the contributions of African-Americans and other groups to the region and displays contemporary life in the region (e.g. stock car racing). These new approaches developed out of a shift in intellectual history during this same time period that foregrounded marginalized cultures, revisions in traditional historical accounts, and such notions as the invention of tradition and cultural hegemony. These ideas altered the character of tourism in Appalachia in ways still influential in the 1990s.

The national parks began and continue to reassess their approaches to interpreting Appalachian culture. Cultural resource studies are helping the parks find ways to reinvent old sites; for example, at the site of the old community of Mons, mentioned earlier, new interpretive materials will restore for the tourist, if not the physical buildings of the community, a mental construct of its former life. The Great Smoky Mountain National Park plans a new visitor center that hopes to tell a more varied and accurate story of the development of the Appalachian region. Many of these new efforts use planning strategies that involve government personnel, scholars in Appalachian Studies, business leaders, and community residents, and seem to be producing far better results. There is now an Appalachian Tourism Research and Development Center in the region devoted to improving our approaches to tourism in the mountains.[2]

Conclusions

Tourism will continue to be a dominant factor in economic development of the Appalachian region for years to come. In parts of the region where the traditional economic base is no longer viable (e.g., parts of the coal field areas, the decline in tobacco-based agriculture in Tennessee and elsewhere), tourism is often seen as the answer to a community's economic woes. But critical study of tourism in Appalachia demonstrates that its effects on the region's culture will continue to have mixed results. Tourism may add dollars to the economy but in low-paying, seasonal jobs with little long-term benefit for local residents. Tourism likely will add to problems of congestion, environmental pollution, and visual blight. Tourism may introduce visitors to Appalachian culture but offer them a skewed picture of the culture that reinforces romantic or negative stereotypes. As one report on tourism in the Appalachian mountains concluded: "Failure to recognize and plan for the costs of tourism not only overstates the benefits but can result in unexpected economic dilemmas and decrease the quality of life in a community. Ultimately, these problems can be detrimental to the tourism industry and those dependent on it..." (Dockery 1991).

A recent trend in studies of the Appalachian region is comparative study of Appalachia and other mountain regions of the world on issues of environmental concern, economic development, tourism, and cultural concerns. Scholars in Appalachia have looked to Norway, Italy, Germany, Nepal, and elsewhere for such comparisons. For example, one study explores the similarities between Appalachia and the Mezzogiorno in southern Italy, especially their social and economic conditions, and the Cassa per il Mezzogiorno in Italy and the Appalachian Regional Commission in the United States (Obermiller 1992). Other

Appalachian scholars have conducted fieldwork in Galicia in Spain, in Bavaria, in the hill country of the British Isles, and a host of other mountain settings. What we are confirming is that "the rest of the world's population has always looked to the mountains for sustenance—for water, for wood, for minerals, and for a host of other resources. The mountain people themselves, however, have traditionally been feared or revered, but scarcely understood" (Tobias 1986). Mountain people worldwide have been alternately romanticized or denigrated while the richness of their land has been exploited, often in direct relationship.

More and more we are learning how fragile are our mountain areas and the cultures that have arisen in them. Collectively, we recognize what Jack Ives has said so well:

> Mountain landscapes and mountain people are best characterized by their infinite variety and great complexity. Despite a rapidly increasing research effort, they remain virtually unknown. All generalizations but two are both difficult and dangerous, if not downright irresponsible. The exceptions: that they are under enormous pressure and that change through "development" will occur. The more effectively such development can be based on a full understanding of the behavior patterns and perceptions of the mountain people, the greater will be the opportunity to reduce unnecessary damage. All of us—scientists, artists, bureaucrats, politicians, and citizens alike—face an obligation to help reduce the damage (Ives 1986).

New approaches to tourism need to be part of the international agenda for sensitive mountain environments. Tourism that respects the cultural integrity, as well as the natural environment, of a mountain region must be our focus. We are searching for ways "to reduce the damage" in Appalachia. Worldwide, we need to share our successes and failures.

Notes

[1]For a complete study of the site, see Speer et al. 1990.

[2]The Appalachian Tourism Research and Development Center is affiliated with Concord College and West Virginia University; address is Concord College, Box D-137, Athens, West Virginia 24712, USA.

References

Dockerey, Bill (1991) "Reports on Tourism." *Now and Then, the Appalachian Magazine* 8 (Spring):41.

Dunn, Durwood (1988) *Cades Cove: The Life and Death of a Southern Appalachian Community, 1818–1973*. Knoxville: University of Tennessee Press.

Fox, John, Jr (1909) *A Mountain Europa*. New York: Charles Scribner's Sons.

Harney, Will Wallace (1873) "A Strange Land and Peculiar People." *Lippincott's Magazine* 12 (October):429–38.

Ives, Jack (1986) "Introduction: The Future of the Earth's Mountains." In *Mountain People* (edited by Tobias, Michael), 15. Norman: University of Oklahoma Press.

Obermiller, Phillip J. (1992) "From the Apennines to Appalachia: New Strategy Needed." *Appalachian Heritage* 20 (Summer):30–42.

Reclus, Elise (1881) *The History of a Mountain*. New York: Harper and Brothers.

Speer, Jean Haskell, Frances Russell and Gibson Worsham (1990) *The Johnson Farm at Peaks of Otter*. Asheville: Blue Ridge Parkway/National Park Service.

Tobias, Michael, ed. (1986) *Mountain People*. Norman: University of Oklahoma Press.

7

BUILDING BLOCKS FOR NEW ECONOMIC OPPORTUNITIES: NATIONAL REGISTER PROJECTS AT THE MTSU CENTER FOR HISTORIC PRESERVATION

CARROLL VAN WEST

"Tourism is fast becoming the biggest industry in the world, 'The Greatest Show on Earth.' The life blood of much of that industry is heritage," recently observed Priscilla Boniface and Peter J. Fowler (Boniface and Fowler 1993). In their search to enhance the stability and economic vitality of their downtown business districts and to diversify their economic base, local governments and chambers of commerce have turned to heritage tourism as a way to improve community pride, identity, and economic development. Heritage tourism means many different things to many different people, but, in general, the term refers to an economic development strategy grounded in attracting tourists and tourist-spend dollars.[1] The distinctiveness of a community, as represented in its historic buildings, places, and traditions, provides useful building blocks for the future, for a place without a collective identity finds it difficult to maintain stability and a sense of shared purpose in facing the social and economic challenges of modern life. In today's increasingly homongenized and standardized landscape, people—especially the traveling public—are drawn to distinctive cultures and places. Heritage tourism programs and projects are designed to identify, preserve, and enhance the culturally defining characteristics of a community and then to market them to the large number of interstate, and intrastate, tourists that travel American interstates and highways.

Tennessee communities have embraced the concept of heritage tourism for many decades. An impetus behind the creation of Shiloh Military Park in Hardin County one hundred years ago was how local entrepreneurs could benefit from the expected visitors. The Great Smoky Mountains National Park had as many businessmen supporting it as there were conservationists.[2] Potential economic benefits attracted support for the preservation of Andrew Jackson's Hermitage as early as 1889. Women members of the Ladies Hermitage Association regularly addressed commercial and professional conferences in Nashville as part of a coordinated effort to convince visitors that Nashville was a distinctive, attractive place, worthy of investment and a vacation day or two. The same

Table 1. Tennessee Communities
Participating in the Main Street
Program, 1983–1993.

Town	Date Program Established
Brownsville	1983
Columbia	1983
Gallatin	1983
Greeneville	1983
Pulaski	1983
Covington	1985
Franklin	1985
Kingsport	1985
Murfreesboro	1985
Bristol	1986
Elizabethton	1986
Fayetteville	1990
Sparta	1990
Collierville	1990
Cleveland	1990
Union City	1990

Source: Data from Tennessee Main Street Program, Tennessee Department of Economic and Community.

economic argument for historic preservation was made by the Knoxville women's group who restored Blount Mansion in Knoxville during the 1920s.[3] In an article titled, "Preservation of Blount Home Would Be Business Asset to This Section," in the *Knoxville News* of 25 February 1926, Mrs B.B. Cates predicted that the house "will attract many tourists, for they will go miles out of their way to see things of historical interest."[4]

These basic assumptions about heritage tourism have not changed in seventy years, but the roots of the current interest in heritage tourism lie in more recent developments and programs, especially the successful Main Street Program, initially established by the National Trust for Historic Preservation. The desire to create an attractive facade for downtown business districts was an important component of the Tennessee Main Street Program, which was established in 1983 with support from the National Park Service, the Tennessee Historical Commission and the National Trust for Historic Preservation. The Main Street Program has touched all parts of the state (see Table 1). During the program's first five years, almost $2.3 million in private and public funds were invested in rehabilitation and promotional projects; over 500 buildings were rehabilitated and put to new uses and 1,677 new jobs were created. As of late 1993, these numbers had increased to over $120 million dollars of private and public investment and over 2,700 new jobs have been created.[5] Both business leaders and local government officials learned that preservation and historic architecture paid off in both a more attractive and a more economically productive downtown business district.

Not surprisingly then, Main Street communities—already cognizant of the potential positive economic interrelationship between historic preservation and downtown revitalization—have been among the leaders of the heritage tourism initiative in Tennessee. Other significant contributors have included the Certified Local Government program of the Tennessee Historical Commission and the Center for Historic Preservation at Middle Tennessee State University. Clearly the most important support has come from the Tennessee Department of Tourist

Development. With this statewide infrastructure in place, "Main Street" towns like Greenville and Kingsport jumped at the chance to become involved when the National Trust for Historic Preservation launched its Heritage Tourism initiative in 1990.[6] This program, organized by the National Trust and reliant on support from the National Endowment for the Arts and state departments of tourism, chose Tennessee as one of the first four pilot projects, due to the success of the earlier Trust-supported Main Street program and the presence of a strong statewide infrastructure composed of the earlier mentioned agencies and university departments. Throughout the pilot project period, the Department of Tourist Development especially provided much assistance and expertise to the four pilot areas. Northeast Tennessee (thematically named "America's First Frontier), Southeast Tennessee ("Tennessee Overhill Country"), Southcentral Tennessee ("Tennessee's Backroads Heritage"), and western Middle Tennessee ("Tennessee Natchez Trace Corridor") were the four regions that eventually launched successful programs. "Some initial difficulty was encountered in uniting the varied country and city governments involved in these multi-county heritage tourism alliances," admitted the directors of the southcentral Tennessee program, "but hesitancy is being overcome in favor of the obvious advantages of unity." They concluded: "it has been proven that a region has more impact if it speaks with one voice, recognizes its common heritage, protects its historic fabric, and cooperates to promote the entire area" (Hulan and Johnson 1992).

As the state's Main Street Program continued to expand in 1989–1990, at the same time that the new Heritage Tourism initiative was beginning to make its mark, the Center for Historic Preservation at Middle Tennessee State University found itself answering many calls for assistance from Tennessee communities. The Center for Historic Preservation was among the first group of Centers of Excellence, established by the state legislature in 1984. From its inception, its goals have included the identification, protection, conservation, and interpretation of Tennessee's historic resources as well as providing strategies that provide for the continued use and economic enhancement of these historic buildings and places. Drawing from the analysis and recommendations contained in its 1988 National Trust-commissioned report on the region and its resources, *The Best of Both Worlds: The Challenge of Growth Enhancement in the Mid-South* (Van West 1988), Center staff developed a multi-faceted response, based on a building block approach to a community's needs in historic preservation and economic development.[7]

The first building block was for the Center to assess the historic places and properties of a community and then to work with property owners and community leaders to nominate these properties to the National Register of Historic Places. The National Register is "the nation's official list of historic properties worth preserving" (Interagency Resources Division 1991:ix). Listing in the National Register automatically gives a historic house or place more credibility with the traveling public because the property has met national standards for

significance in history and historic architecture. Towns and individual businesses often highlight their National Register status in publicity and in highway
advertising signs. The Jack Daniels corporation, for example, has long highlighted its National Register-listed distillery at Lynchburg on advertising signs
along Interstate I-24; officials recently worked with the author to list Mary
Bobo's Boardinghouse, another Jack Daniels-owned historic property in
Lynchburg.[8] More importantly, listing in the National Register makes properties eligible for historic preservation tax credits, federal preservation funds (when
available), and other economic incentives.[9]

Due to high demand for its services, the Center has developed a list of criteria to guide its selection of National Register projects. The first consideration is
need, which is determined by looking at three related questions: 1) does this
community lack the necessary staff and financial resources to produce National Register nominations? 2) does the town need a potential economic boost
from heritage tourism or preservation financial benefits? 3) are its historic resources threatened by economic decline, neglect, or possible demolition?

The next consideration is *support*, which is measured by a set of four related
questions: 1) are local property owners interested in the National Register program? 2) is this proposal supported by the local Chamber of Commerce (or
similar group), Main Street Program (if one is in place), and local government
officials? 3) does the request have the prior support of such state and federal
agencies as the state regional development districts, the department of tourism,
the Tennessee Historical Commission, or the Tennessee Valley Authority? 4)
how strong is the likelihood that after the National Register work is completed,
local citizens, businessmen, and governmental officials will work together to
build upon the preservation foundation and actually enhance and use their historic resources?

The final criterion is *historical significance*. We carefully consider the community's past and its remaining historic resources: 1) does the community have
properties that meet the eligibility requirements of the National Register? 2)
does it have places that would add significant historical information to neglected periods or themes in Tennessee history (such as African-American history)? 3) does the county already have many properties listed in the National
Register? Our preference is to give first consideration to counties and themes
that are under-represented in the statewide National Register program.

With this set of selection criteria in mind, from 1989 to 1991 the Center for
Historic Preservation selected three different pilot projects, representing all
three grand divisions of Tennessee. The first came in 1989, at Cumberland Gap,
in Claiborne County. Claiborne County then had ten properties listed in the
National Register, two of which were connected to the adjacent Cumberland
Gap National Historical Park, which is administered by the National Park Serv-
ice. Surprisingly, the actual town of Cumberland Gap had nothing listed in the
National Register, even though the town had designated a local historic district

in 1979. Local officials realized that without the National Register listing, nothing in the town would be eligible for federal financial assistance. In addition, economic development experts at the Tennessee Valley Authority had already selected Cumberland Gap as a perfect place to take advantage of a cultural tourism initiative.[10] As early as 1986, TVA and the National Trust for Historic Preservation had co-sponsored a regional workshop titled "Bringing Tourists to Town: How Historic Resources Can Help" which was held at Morristown, Tennessee. The Tennessee Historical Commission also was interested in the project and a representative from that agency attended the initial planning meeting, along with representatives from the Center, TVA, the National Park Service, local government officials, and local property owners. Due to the town's interesting history as a planned industrial village from 1890 to 1930, Cumberland Gap met all three of the Center's criteria for a National Register project: need, support, and historical significance.

Because the three criteria were met, the Center agreed to conduct the National Register nomination as a public service and graduate student training project. Only the actual expenses for travel, film, and supplies would be charged. In that way, the Center leverages its funding from the state legislature to produce high-quality but low cost assistance for the historic preservation and economic development of Tennessee communities. At the same time, it provides MTSU students who desire an education in historic preservation with a realistic and worthwhile fieldwork experience that provides them with valuable professional training for their future careers.

As the nomination was being completed and officially listed in the National Register in 1990, the city of Cumberland Gap and the Tennessee Valley Authority went to work, placing advertising signs listing the town's National Register status on the adjacent federal highway and developing historic walking tours for those tourists attracted to the town. Working with "Sight Through Helping Hands" from Austin, Texas, they even developed an innovative braille trail for the blind.[11]

The success at Cumberland Gap encouraged the Center to tackle a much larger Tennessee town for its next pilot project. Dyersburg (population 16,317 in 1990), the seat of Dyer County, is the largest town north of Jackson in West Tennessee. But in 1990 Dyersburg and the entire Dyer County had only three individual properties listed in the National Register. Chamber of Commerce officials, however, wanted to help local business owners in the downtown business district to take advantage of preservation financial incentives and to establish a more attractive destination for the increasing number of tourists passing through Dyer County. At the invitation of the Chamber, Center staff first spoke to a public meeting to promote the values of historic preservation and cultural tourism before any National Register work took place. The opportunity to assess public opinion and the depth of commitment from civic and business groups proved valuable in the future development of the project. A story about the public meeting was the lead headline on the front page of the next day's newspaper and positive media coverage was another source of strength throughout the Dyersburg project. Since that time, the Center has always attempted to hold public information meetings about its National Register projects before any actual work begins; the ideas and recommendations of community and business leaders are welcomed throughout the process (Whittle 1989).

A team of MTSU graduate students, supervised by Center staff, tackled the historic districts and neighborhoods of Dyersburg in early 1990. Over the next two years, the Center used this research to develop three separate historic districts, the first being the downtown business district, followed next by two residential neighborhoods. The author and his graduate assistant Jennifer Martin Maxwell also developed a National Register "Multiple Property Cover Form," which provided a comprehensive architectural and historical overview of local historic resources, enabling property owners in the future to nominate eligible buildings to the National Register of Historic Places by placing their individual property information into the context already established by the multiple property cover form. In late December, 1991, staff from the Center for Historic Preservation and the Tennessee Historical Commission held a final public meeting to present the results of the project and to explain the benefits of National Register listing to local property owners (Whittle 1989).

Working with a broad partnership of state and local government officials, the local Chamber of Commerce, and individual citizens, the Center for Historic Preservation was able to provide Dyersburg with a historic preservation infrastructure that gives city officials and property owners the ability to develop their own economic development and heritage tourism programs, at their own pace, and to meet their own selected needs and goals. Economic solutions are not imposed from outsiders; rather locals may take the historic preservation foundation and build the heritage enhancement projects that best fit their vision for the community.

The success of the Dyersburg project brought the work of the Center to the attention of several other West Tennessee communities. In Dyer County, the Center worked with City of Newbern officials to place Newbern's 1920 Illinois Central Railroad depot on the National Register. It is one of only two Amtrak stops in Tennessee and one of the state's best examples of a successful Heritage Tourism project in a small rural town. In Tipton County, the City of Covington, the Tipton County Historical Society, and its Main Street program worked with the Center in 1991 and 1992 to list the historic Ruffin Theater in the National Register as well as a downtown residential district along South Main Street.

Closer to home, the Center also began to work with the City of Sparta and the Sparta/White County Chamber of Commerce in 1990 on a series of historic preservation and cultural tourism projects. White County is on the divide of the Eastern Highland Rim and the Cumberland Plateau. Like many counties in this region, it is looking for new economic opportunities while maintaining a fierce pride of place. In 1990, White County had only three historic properties listed in the National Register with none located in the central business or residential districts of Sparta, the county seat. Again, public meetings were held at the outset to gauge the depth of community support and commitment. A class of graduate students conducted the initial field research and out of this work, a downtown residential district, a historic theater, a railroad depot, and a historic electric company office have been listed in the National Register, providing Sparta with a historic preservation infrastructure for its recently established Main Street program. This brief summary does not mean to suggest that the historic preservation efforts of the Center and its associated local governments and chambers of commerce have not met with difficulties along the way. Center staff have had spirited but professional debates about the National Register eligibility of certain properties and districts with staff at the Tennessee Historical Commission. Local groups have not developed education programs to inform residents about the value and significance of their historic places as quickly as desired. Consistent funding sources for rehabilitation work have been difficult for small towns to establish and maintain.

But, in general, the Center concluded that the pilot projects had been positive contributions to the preservation and enhancement of Tennessee communities. They used the professional expertise of Center staff to identify and nominate to the National Register significant properties of Tennessee history and architecture. Using these nominations as a foundation, communities could then call upon other Center programs, economic development programs of the state and federal governments, and their own initiative, to establish effective plans for historic preservation and heritage tourism.

Acknowledgements

The author acknowledges the helpful comments of his colleagues James K. Huhta and Caneta S. Hankins in the preparation of this essay.

Notes

[1]For the diversity of meanings and interpretations, see "Giving Our Past..." 1987; Economic Research Associates 1989; Horowitz 1986; Lew 1985; the Summer 1994 issue of *Touchstone*, the newsletter of the Tennessee Humanities Council, features a special focus on "cultural tourism" in Tennessee. That two terms, "Heritage Tourism" and "Cultural Tourism," are both used to describe similar projects and concerns is largely a semantic difference. Professionals involved in either program, whether historians, preservationists, anthropologists, folklorists, museum officials, or tourism promoters, direct their efforts to bringing new recognition and economic choices to communities by interpreting and enhancing the artifacts of the community's collective identity, history, and culture.

[2]On the entire issue of tourism and Appalachia, particularly see Duggan 1990 and Howell 1990. On-going research by Dan Pierce and Bren Martin, graduate students in history at the University of Tennessee, Knoxville, provides particularly valuable data about the relationship between early twentieth-century economic development and Appalachian tourism. Also see Dunn 1990:201–40 and Jolley 1969:9–44.

[3]For the twentieth century fascination of travelers with historic things and places, see, in general, Jakle 1985; see early story supporting the preservation of the Hermitage in "Hermitage Memorial Association" 1889; Bucy 1995; Whitworth 1989:24.

[4]The newspaper story is quoted in Whitworth 1989:24.

[5]"Down on Main Street" 1993. The program is part of the Tennessee Department of Economic and Community Development, Rachel Jackson Office Building, Sixth Floor, Nashville, TN 37243-0405.

[6]A useful way of assessing this program is through its quarterly newsletter, *Heritage Tourism Update*, published by the Denver Regional Office of the National Trust for Historic Preservation from 1990 to 1993.

[7]The program discussed in this article is only one of many responses the Center has developed to meet the demand for cultural tourism assistance. In 1993, for example, Center staff guided a group of graduate students in producing "Old South Charm, New South Progress: Heritage Tourism in Maury County: A Heritage Tourism Plan" (Murfreesboro, 1993). This was a comprehensive guidebook to heritage tourism in one country, prepared for the local Chamber of Commerce, and designed to help the county plan for the conversion of a National Register-listed antebellum mansion, Rippa Villa, into a tourism visitor center. The Saturn Corporation has since transferred Rippa Villa for this new use. Director James K. Huhta and Projects Coordinator Caneta S. Hankins have both played significant leadership roles in developing the agenda for heritage tourism in Tennessee; in particular their work with the state Main Street Program and the Heritage Tourism pilot projects.

[8]*Tullahoma News and Guardian*, 28 January 1994; *Moore County News*, 4 February 1994.

[9]Blumenthal 1990:49–53 lists the appropriate IRS regulations for preservation tax incentives.

[10]Since its inception, the Tennessee Valley Authority has provided economic development assistance to communities within its large service region.

[11]The project is discussed in "Spring Projects..." 1989

References

Blumenthal, Sara K., comp. (1990). *Federal Historic Preservation Laws*. Washington DC.

Boniface, Priscilla and Peter J. Fowler (1993) *Heritage and Tourism in 'The Global Village'*. London and New York.

Bucy, Carole S. (1995) "Quite Revolutionaries: The Grundy Women and the Beginnings of Women Volunteer Associations in Tennessee." Annual Lindsley Lecture, Tennessee Historical Society, Nashville TN, November 1993. *Tennessee Historical Quar-*

terly (Spring).

"Down on Main Street" (1993) *Tennessee Preservationist* 2(1):1,5.

Duggan, Betty J. 1990. "New Ways for Old: Assessing Contributions of the Tennessee Community Heritage Project." In *Cultural Heritage Conservation in the American South* (edited by Howell, Benita J.), 54–65. Athens, GA.

Dunn, Durwood (1988). *Cades Cove: The Life and Death of a Southern Appalachian Community, 1818–1937*. Knoxville.

Economic Research Associates (1989) *National Policy Study of Rural Tourism and Small Business Develoopment*. N.p.: United States Travel and Tourism Administration.

"Giving Our Past A Future." (1987) *Heritage Communicator* 1 (October):18.

"Hermitage Memorial Association" (1889) *Nashville Daily American*, 15 February.

Horowitz, Amy L. (1986) "Developing a Tourism Program." *Main Street News* (February):1–2.

Howell, Benita J. 1990. "AppalachianTourism and Cultural Conservation." In *Cultural Heritage Conservation in the American South* (edited by Howell, Benita J.), 125–39. Athens, GA.

Hulan, Lynn and Wanda Johnson (1992) "Historic Preservation and Heritage Tourism." *Tennessee Preservationist* 1(2):1.

Interagency Resources Division, National Park Service, et al. (1991) *National Register of Historic Places, 1966–1991*. Nashville TN.

Jakle, John A. (1985). *The Tourist: Travel in Twentieth-Century North America*. Lincoln : University of Nebraska Press.

Jolley, Harley E. (1969) *The Blue Ridge Parkway*. Knoxville.

Lew, Alan A. (1985) "Bringing Tourists to Town." *Small Town* (July–August):4–10.

"Spring Projects in East Tennessee: Cumberland Gap" (1989). *Center for Historic Preservation Newsletter* (May):1–2.

Van West, Carole, ed. (1988) *The Best of Both Worlds: The Challenge of Growth Enhancement in the Mid-South*. Report funded by a Critical Issues Fund Grant, National Trust for Historic Preservation. Murfreesboro TN.

Whittle, Donna (1989) "Historian: City `something special." *Dyersburg State Gazette*, 8 September, 1, 4.

Whitworth, S. Kent (1989). *Promoting the Tennessee Historical Site*. MA thesis, Middle Tennessee State University, 1989.

8

BLACKFEET CULTURAL AND ECONOMIC DEVELOPMENT THROUGH TRIBAL ARTS: A SURVEY OF PIKUNI ARTISTS

FRANCESCA MCLEAN

Introduction

If you take the Wolf Creek exit off of I-15, follow Route 287 to Highway 89, and turn north you will find yourself running parallel to some of the most breath-taking scenery in America, the eastern front range of the Rocky Mountains. When you reach Birch Creek, you've reached the southern border of the Blackfeet Reservation. The Blackfeet call these mountains "the backbone of the world," easy to understand when you see them, and easy to understand when you know that the stegosaurus spikes of their peaks rise to between 10,000 and 14,000 feet above the foothills and prairies of central Montana. They tower above the Montana landscape and form the spine of the inter-mountain West as well as the hub of the *Pikuni* world.

The *Pikuni* (Piegan, Poor Robes), the Blackfeet of Montana, is one of three bands in a confederacy that includes the Bloods (Kainah, Many Chiefs) and the Northern Blackfeet (Siksika, Blackfeet), both of whom reside in the province of Alberta, separated from the Blackfeet by the political boundary of the 49th parallel, the US-Canadian border. The Pikuni nation has approximately 14,000 enrolled members with over half that number living on the reservation. There are over one and a half million acres of land within the boundaries of the reservation; almost 950,000 acres are owned in trust status by individual Indians or by the Tribe, with 38% owned by non-Indians. In this rural landscape the population density is only four persons per square mile.

Tribal unemployment is approximately 64% for the full year, and rises to 85% during the winter. Yet because the reservation is bordered to the west by the eastern entrance to Glacier National Park, close to two million people pass through the reservation each year. This dichotomy in numbers makes clear how little economic benefit the Blackfeet reap from the tourism dollars that are spent on or near the reservation each year.

The Project

Several years ago my predecessor as Director of Folklife Programs for the Montana Arts Council, Nicholas Vrooman, worked with a group of Blackfeet artists and cultural leaders to assess their cultural and economic needs. Together they developed a project that begins to address these needs. The Blackfeet Cultural and Economic Development through Tribal Arts Project was funded by the National Endowment for the Arts as part of their mandate to fund projects in "underserved communities." During FY 95/96 the first phase of the project has been completed and the second phase will be underway soon.

In the spring of 1995, two Blackfeet fieldworkers worked to identify and document Blackfeet artists on or near the reservation. Leonda Fast Buffalo Horse, a Blackfeet artist who works in stained glass, quill and other media, and Kenny Weatherwax, student of tribal culture and history, were contracted part-time for sixteen weeks to identify Blackfeet artists and culture keepers, document their skills and knowledge, access their needs and identify as many repositories of information regarding tribal arts, artists and cultural information as possible, both on and off the reservation. They also researched and compiled archival material on Blackfeet arts and artists, and Fast Buffalo Horse designed and implemented a database containing this information. This essay presents the preliminary results of their survey.

The Survey

To introduce the importance of this project for the tribe, I borrow the words of Blackfeet artists compiled by Fast Buffalo Horse for this project. In a cover letter attached to the "Fieldwork Data Sheet and Project Form" the narrative states:

> Art is integral to our lives, not a career choice. There is no separation of being Blackfeet and being a Blackfeet artist. Everyone is presumed to have creative abilities. "Artist" acknowledgement comes from someone displaying better abilities at certain activities.

> There is a critical need to protect and encourage tribal cultural identity through the reenforcement of tribal members being involved in the production of tribal arts and cultural programming.

> Cultural tourism offers us the opportunity to develop and manage the natural and cultural resources and experiences in such a way that our integrity is conserved and preserved, rather than exploited. The Blackfeet people, because of our proximity to Glacier National Park and our place in the cultural history of America, have an immense amount to offer but reap little of the total economic benefit of tourism in dollars. The Blackfeet people hold a central position in the rise of cultural tourism and the desire for authentic experience, in replacement of sheer entertainment.

The Blackfeet voice needs to be part of the education of the commercial sector of the surrounding areas. Although there is an increasing awareness of the sensitivity to the issue, "Indian" arts and crafts sold in and around Glacier are for the most part non-Indian made, or not representative of Blackfeet or Northern Plains Indian Culture.

We have a strong cultural arts community but need direction and assistance. We need a centralized work area for artists to create; development of standards for high-quality arts production; we need to learn the business of cultural arts supply and demand. We need a place where training of tribal people in the arts can occur. We need a place where cultural performance, arts, and ceremonies can take place, for both private tribal and public cultural tourism events. *We need a wide scope cultural facility.*

The Blackfeet people have received seed money for Phase I of the three phase grant from the National Endowment for the Arts and the Montana Arts Council to document the cultural talents and abilities of the Blackfeet People.

Phase I of this grant is critical (for) all other aspects of cultural work to occur if we are to get a *cultural facility*. The Blackfeet people must know who among us hold what cultural knowledge and skills; who is willing to become arts and cultural program producers; who is keeping valued knowledge and skills alive. This information is needed for both cultural preservation and to demonstrate the viability of future project development.

This documentation is the foundation for a strategy to build a cultural resource/ market data base, business, training and funding relationships and a comprehensive, high-level fund-raising package to position the Blackfeet people for getting additional financial resources to accomplish the long-range goals of building a *cultural facility*.

We hope that you will take a serious interest in this project and give your support by taking the time to complete the following questionnaire. Perhaps together we can accomplish what a few cannot.

This narrative highlights key points both of Blackfeet culture and of the project itself:

- the integral role of art in Blackfeet life;
- protection and control over the production of tribal arts and cultural identity;
- the prospect of economic gain through control and marketing of tribal arts in the cultural tourism market;
- and the need for assistance and education regarding the structure and demands of the marketplace.

The field and research-based organization of the first phase of the project provides a foundation in which to meet these goals and begin the groundwork for building a cultural facility.

Approximately seventy individuals filled out and returned survey forms. The form contained thirteen questions designed to illicit such basic information as: the type of work the artist creates, a list of materials used and the cost of these materials; the cost of the finished pieces; the details of the artists learning methods; and performance specific questions regarding genres and outfit making.

Crucial to the next phase of the project was that part of the survey dealing with economic strategies and what aspects or areas the artists wanted to know more about. The categories were: advertising, pricing their work, pricing structure in the marketplace (both retail and wholesale), retail sales, catalogue marketing, grant writing, product photography, consignment and commission, and copyright/intellectual property issues. Those completing the survey were asked to circle all of the categories about which they wanted more information or in which they would like training.

Interestingly enough, grant writing evoked the highest response (23), with pricing their work a close second (20). Copyright issues ranked third (17) and retail marketing, fourth (16). With regards to grant writing, I fear I will have to explain that the availability of sources of federal grant money for the arts is currently undergoing drastic change. The issues of pricing, retail marketing and copyright may be able to be addressed in workshop formats in cooperation with the other project partners—the Small Business Administration (SBA) and/ or the state of Montana's Department of Commerce, the National Park Service at Glacier National Park, and the Montana Rural Development Council.

While these partners have only been marginally involved to date, there is already trouble afoot. The reputation of the Park Service, Glacier Park International and the SBA on the reservation is poor at best. Park Service rangers have designed and coordinated cultural programs at the lodges and campgrounds around the Park for the last fifteen years. They have worked with many members of the tribe, hiring dancers, singers, storytellers and others to present Blackfeet culture to the tourists. They have developed good working relationships with some and generated tensions with others. It is important politically to know that Park land was once Blackfeet land and remains culturally important to the tribe. Blackfeet attorneys and council members often wrangle with Park officials regarding Blackfeet land use within park boundaries.

Furthermore, there is a great deal of resentment towards the park's major vending company, Glacier Park International (a subsidiary of the Dial company). The buying policies, practices and timelines of the corporation remain unclear to many Blackfeet artists. Second-hand reports of unfair treatment and buying policies abound. The vendors do their buying only in April, for the entire season. Glacier Park International's price structure is different from the Northern Plains Crafts Cooperative, the other major purchaser on the reservation, and artists often feel that they are being paid less than they deserve, especially when they see the retail price for which their goods are sold. Authentic Blackfeet art and jewelry also compete with foreign-made imitations without the benefit of clear differentiation made between the two at the point of purchase.

Another major source of tension lies in the tribe's relationship with the SBA. Chief Old Person tells me that over the years the SBA has sent any number of people to work with different projects on the reservation. Consistently, whenever tribal members develop a good working relationship with an agency staff member, the agency almost immediately stops allowing them to continue on the project in question and sends someone else, thus destroying any continuity, trust or real ability to get good work done on the reservation. This current economic development project is no exception.

Nora Walsh, the supervisor of the economic development section, accompanied me on several trips to the reservation and had almost instant rapport with various tribal members, including Chief Old Person. As soon as her supervisor learned of Walsh's success with the Blackfeet, she made it impossible for Walsh to return to the reservation. Once again, the SBA has reinforced the tribe's negative experience, jeopardized a segment of the development project and made things difficult for the tribe (and for me) within this project. Politically I am unable to remove them from the project; practically I am striving to get some useful contribution from them while lessening their negative presence.

These situations with Glacier Park International and the SBA exemplify the cultural differences between the Blackfeet and the non-Indian communities with which they do business. Among these difference are communication styles, value judgements regarding both the monetary and cultural value of a piece of jewelry or art, and the key importance of establishing trusted and on-going relationships. Non-Indian people do not seem to understand the amount of time and artistic talent it takes to make the beautiful beaded piece that are central to Blackfeet artistic traditions. Part way through the survey fieldwork, Leonda Fast Buffalo Horse called to tell me that people were having a great deal of trouble on the question that asked them to price their work. Most Indian artists cannot make a living from their work. Thus they hold down full-time jobs and do their creative work in their spare time. Five minutes here and an hour or two there over the course of a week or more add up to a finished piece. Within this necessarily flexible work schedule—artists usually have a family and household to tend to as well—it was extremely hard for them to determine how much time it takes in total to complete a piece. I asked Fast Buffalo Horse if she and some of the other artists surveyed could keep a log of the hours it took for several pieces and then determine how much their time and talents were worth. This determination, plus the cost of materials, plus a knowledge of what the retail market will bear should allow artists to price their work fairly.

Culturally, the work style of Blackfeet artists and the organizational structure required to generate the necessary information to price their work are at odds. Cultural differences in accessing value also increase tensions. The value of an artist's time can be more easily understood by a business community. The value of talent is also culturally assigned and thus often misunderstood, and both of these factors and more are balanced against profit margins and price points. Assigning value to personal, face-to-face communication that continues through the years is also difficult for those who work in the often transient world of corporate America. People are identified by their job titles, and as long as someone in the corporation is fulfilling the function of the job, the corporation is satisfied. Culturally, Indian people find this strange because the success or failure of a relationship developed with someone from a corporation or public agency depends a great deal on the personal credibility and trustworthiness of the individual involved.

In spite of cross-cultural communication problems, the momentum of the project remains strong and the good work continues. The challenges ahead are many. We must find funds to meet the long- and short -term goals of the project. We must mediate between Indian and non-Indian groups who must share the land and cooperate for successful marketing of both the region and Blackfeet art and culture. We must cultivate support to create a lasting and positive economic and cultural impact for the Blackfeet Nation, and to build a cultural center where both work and celebration can take place. Hopefully, in the process the Blackfeet will create a model that can be used by other tribes and other business communities to their own benefit.

Acknowledgements

I would like to thank Chief Earl Old Person, Chairman of the Blackfeet Tribal Business Council, and all the Council members, for their on-going support of this project. Advisors to this project include: Jackie Parsons, Darrell Norman, Curley Bear Wagner, Feral Wagner, Joyce Spoonhunter, Bill Farr and Nora Walsh. Without their assistance, and the continued support of Blackfeet artists specifically, and many other members of the Blackfeet nation, this project would have suffered considerably. Financial support for this project was provided by a grant from the National Endowment for the Arts; the Montana Arts, the Blackfeet Nation, the Small Business Administration and the National Park Service also contributed time and expertise.

9

HERITAGE TOURISM: A TOOL FOR ECONOMIC DEVELOPMENT

LINDA CALDWELL

In the southeast corner of Tennessee lies a pocket of land that was once home to the Cherokee Overhill Towns. Mountains and hills rise from the valleys of the Ocoee, Hiwassee, Tellico and Little Tennessee rivers. These rivers, along with overland trails, once carried furs and hides to Charleston, South Carolina, where they were shipped to Europe, a brisk trade that introduced the Overhill to the world market.

The Overhill was blessed with abundant natural resources. Copper, gold, timber, water and cheap labor made the region very attractive to developers and New South boosters between 1850 and the turn of the century. People from everywhere poured into new Overhill towns that were built by railroad, lumber, mining and textile companies. One such town was Etowah, built by the Louisville & Nashville Railroad in 1906 as a rail center and township for its workforce. An early resident described Etowah as "a young town—filled with young people with money in their pockets." And Etowah was not alone. Only seven miles up the road, young women also had money in their pockets from working in the textile mills in Englewood. The copper mining towns of Ducktown and Copperhill were filled with miners who made a good wage and enjoyed life in a town where the company provided everything from houses to stores. The sounds of loggers and teamsters could be heard as they at worked in the mountains of Monroe County. Like much of Appalachia, resource extraction was the order of business. But the ores and timber played out or became impractical to extract. As economic patterns shifted, hard times came. While some of the towns were diverse enough to withstand the changes, others suffered and continue to search for solutions and new identities. Currently, although manufacturing jobs are becoming harder to find, there are efforts to create more local industrial jobs. However, many of the Overhill communities do not possess the infrastructure that will allow for any significant industrial growth. People are willing to commute to work at industries, but since people tend to shop where they work, local downtown commercial districts suffer. The coming "information age" offers some economic hope, but there is concern over what to do in the meantime. People in the Overhill could leave the region, but are unwilling to abandon these towns filled with personal meaning for the sons and daughters of miners, loggers, farmers, railroaders and "lintheads." So, they look for solutions and strategies that will allow them to hold on to these special places. Some of the towns are reconciled to the fact that they are no longer important economic centers and are willing to work toward the goal of being good bedroom communities, but they must grapple with ways to pay for services that will offer a desirable quality of life to people who choose to remain or to relocate to the Overhill.

Tourism is one strategy often considered for infusing new dollars into a region or community. In many cases, embarking on a tourism development program results in a plan for promotion rather than development. The Tennessee Department of Tourist Development broke this mold in 1990 when Tennessee was selected as a pilot state for the National Trust for Historic Preservation's Heritage Tourism Initiative. The National Trust, armed with a grant from the National Endowment for the Arts, created the Initiative to partner the tourism industry with the preservation and arts communities to create sustainable, locally controlled tourism programs that focus on development as well as marketing.

Heritage (or cultural) tourism has been defined as showcasing what is unique and special about a place in a way that is agreeable to its residents. Preservation is the first love of the National Trust, but the organization believes that in order for historic sites and museums to find money for preservation and maintenance of historic places, it is important to learn about marketing and business development. The arts and preservation communities have much to offer in return. Travel trends point to an increased interest in visiting historic sites and cultural events. Operators of sites and attractions will benefit from listening to people who are experienced in interpretation and events management.

McMinn, Monroe and Polk Counties became involved with the national program when the region was selected as a Tennessee pilot area. From the local perspective,the timing was perfect. With help from the Tennessee Humanities Council, several communities had finished public history projects that allowed residents to gain fresh insights into the economic history of the region. Informal discussions about ways to market the region's industrial heritage were already underway, and the announcement of this program was greeted with enthusiasm. Calls between small towns and rural museums in the three county region resulted in the decision that the Etowah Arts Commission would prepare a proposal on behalf of McMinn, Monroe and Polk Counties. The Southeast Tennessee Development District provided technical assistance and encouragement. The initial euphoria over the selection of our region as one of the four Tennessee pilot areas was soon replaced by fear that local governments might not embrace the concept or provide the essential funding required to participate in the three year program. But support did come from each county, as well as several municipalities and civic groups. This support, complemented by a grant from the East Tennessee Foundations' Chris Whittle Fund for McMinn County, allowed us to launch the local program. A new organization, governed by people from across the region, was formed and named the region "the Tennessee Overhill," a name used historically for the region prior to Tennessee's statehood.

The first two years of the program were spent on research and training. Consultants from a variety of disciplines assisted the local group with training in such areas as museum development and regional marketing. Surveys on site visitation were completed. A three-year strategic plan was drafted. As we learned more about tourism we began to understand the importance of regionalism. Local people were afraid that a regional approach would cause smaller Overhill attractions to become lost in the shadow of the Tennessee Aquarium or the Smokies. But we soon came to understand that no one attraction or single county possessed the resources for a complete package to sell to tourists. However, a resource inventory made it apparent that outdoor recreation, complemented by museums, historic sites, special events and the services and attractions offered by small towns (shops, eateries and lodging) presented an opportunity to market a mini-regional package that could capture the imagination of travel writers and tourists alike. The region is large enough to provide an assortment of places to see and things to do, yet small enough to cast attention on the specific local attractions that might go unmentioned in promotions done by regions with eight or more counties.

Community education was a challenge. There were people who thought tourism development should not be considered for economic development at all. There were old line tourism types who had little regard for or understanding of heritage tourism. The Overhill Association's first brochure was designed to explain the project and the concept behind it to the indigenous population. A slide show and exhibit were created and then taken on the civic club circuit by members of the Overhill Community Education Committee. Support from the Tennessee Department of Tourism Development was especially helpful at this point. People who thought of tourism development only in terms of billboards, brochures and paid advertising were more comfortable discussing broader approaches to tourism development with a respected agency than with a new and untested organization. The state agency reinforced our efforts on several fronts.

From the beginning the Tennessee Overhill has followed the five principles of heritage tourism that were set forth by the National Trust for Historic Preservation:

1. Focus on authenticity and quality.
2. Preserve and protect resources.
3. Make sites come alive.
4. Find the fit between the community and tourism.
5. Collaborate.

I will briefly discuss how the Tennessee Overhill Project has integrated these principles into our strategies and practices for effective tourism development.

Authenticity and Quality

We are convinced that the true stories of the Overhill are far more interesting than any fictional commercialized version. The Tennessee Arts Commission has recently secured a grant from the National Endowment for the Arts to document and present the folk arts of the Overhill. A professional folk cultural specialist will work with local agencies and organizations (such as museums and theaters) to increase folk arts programming and will provide technical assistance to the Overhill organization and the artists themselves. What does this have to do with tourism development? Everything. Local culture is an underused accessible resource. People from metropolitan areas are not interested in coming to a rural town to see a watered down version of a Broadway play, but they will come to see something unique to that place. Creating events or marketing existing events that showcase local culture can ultimately increase visitation and build community pride. Care must be taken, however, that local history and culture are presented with respect and sensitivity.

Preserving and Protecting Resources

It is important to safeguard the future of tourism by protecting the unique elements that attract visitors initially. The Overhill Advisory Council believes that mismanaged tourism and inappropriate growth would produce a program amounting to another extractive industry. Slower growth, controlled by local people, is more desirable. There is a shortage of tools for local people to use for control. Zoning is an unpopular option, and an argument can be made that resistance to zoning is a local decision. Therefore, we are addressing such concerns subtly through education. An aggressive stance will not work. Several exciting preservation projects are currently underway in the Overhill. One such project is in Etowah, where the city government and the Arts Commission are working together to restore the historic Gem Theater as a public performance space. The city's strategy includes development of programming that will attract visitors as well as local people. Both private and public efforts to preserve special places can be found across the region.

Preservation means more than saving historic buildings or protecting open space—it also means identifying traditional culture and building an appreciation for that which makes our culture unique. There is a economic advantage to cultural tourism: travel and lifestyle writers appreciate story opportunities offered by folk artists, traditional craftsmen and sites that reflect the uniqueness of a region.

Making Sites Come Alive

Thoughtful interpretation can provoke visitors' interest in a region in a way that will result in return visits and opportunities to extend seasons. Many of our communities have taken advantage of the technical assistance offered through the Heritage Tourism Initiative, the Tennessee Humanities Council and the Tennessee Arts Commission to improve the quality of interpretation at museums and historic sites. Englewood's new textile museum is a place to celebrate the history of this mill town. The museum serves a dual purpose: it is a tool to educate visitors and locals and it is also a magnet to attract visitors to the downtown area for shopping and dining. The Ducktown Basin Museum is beginning to revamp its interpretation to provide a better understanding of the history and culture of The Copper Basin and will complete it in time to share the story with the international audience that will be attracted to the nearby Ocoee River for the 1996 Olympic White Water Competition. The Cherokee National Forest is currently working on expanded interpretation of natural and historical resources in the forest.

Finding the Fit

Ensuring that tourism is of economic and *social* benefit to residents. Small local businesses must learn how to capitalize on changing markets. Capital must be found to continue local preservation efforts. For this reason the Overhill has become involved in facets of economic development that are not normally associated with tourism development. Participation in the East Tennessee Community Design Center's Rural Connections II Program helped several small Overhill communities to launch projects designed to increase community income. The East Tennessee Foundation established a small grant program to help Rural Connections participants jump start projects. The Coker Creek Ruritan Club formed an economic development corporation that is reviving the strong crafts heritage of Coker Creek and helping others find ways to increase family income. The Community Action Group of Englewood worked on a feasibility study and pro forma for its museum building and mounted a fund raising campaign for bricks and mortar. Copperhill opened a new visitor center.

The USDA Forest Service and the Cherokee National Forest targeted the Overhill for work through its Economic Recovery Program, which was created to assist communities affected by timber sales. They provided grants for projects ranging from printed collateral materials to market studies and hospitality training. The Forest Service and National Resource Conservation & Development Council also arranged for me to participate in national conferences that provide professional training and a sense of how our local communities fit within the broader context of the issues of national and global land use and economic development.

One frustration is the absence of a state mechanism to provide more help for revitalization of small downtown areas. The National Trust for Historic Preservation's Main Street Program includes strategies that we think could help our towns. Successful Main Street programs produce more than building refurbishment, paint, trees and awnings. A good Main Street program addresses numerous issues including business recruitment, market niches, retail merchandising, and cooperative marketing. However, most Main Street programs are geared for towns with populations greater than 5,000; most Overhill towns have fewer than 5,000 people. It is possible that the current Main Street program would not be effective in places with less critical mass, but a similar program using a comprehensive approach that is specifically geared to small communities is much needed.

Collaborating

Building cooperation between and among business people, operators of historic sites and museums, and governments was the guiding principle for forming the Tennessee Overhill Advisory Council and is the reason the council comprises such diverse people as forest rangers, museum directors, business people, real estate agents, preservationists, civic workers, craftsmen, and local residents.

Much of the success of the Overhill program is due to this group. Our partnership with the Cherokee National Forest and the US Forest Service has been very rewarding to our region. The Cherokee National Forest is our biggest natural resource—a major tourist attraction that we do not spend local monies to maintain. It also provides human resources specialists in rural development, recreation, interpretation, land and water. Our work with the Forest Service grew out of the Heritage Tourism Initiative.

New government partners include TVA, Appalachian Regional Commission, and the Southeast Tennessee Resource & Development Council. Agencies with which we have longstanding relationships, including the Tennessee Arts Commission, Tennessee Humanities Council, Tennessee Department of Tourist Development and the Southeast Tennessee Development District, continue to help us plan for the future. The local government partnership that was created when McMinn, Monroe and Polk Counties agreed to jointly fund the Overhill project was critical. Without basic support for the office and staff it would be difficult to function productively.

The work of the National Trust for Historic Preservation and the Tennessee Department of Tourist Development with McMinn, Monroe and Polk Counties has been even more important that we initially realized. There are new printed materials available to market the Overhill. A new hospitality curriculum is being developed. The Overhill is beginning to enjoy a market identity that is evident in the increased inquires about the region by name. A study grant from the USDA Forest Service was used to contract for the assistance of the National Trust for Historic Preservation in developing a market plan for 1995–1996 that could best capitalize on the 1996 Olympics on the Ocoee River. A new regional organization exists, with an expanded mission that will continue to work toward an holistic approach to economic development. We will continue to consider our past as we plan for the future in the Overhill.

Notes

[1]The experiences of the sixteen pilot areas of the 1989 Heritage Tourism Initiative have been synthesized in the booklet "Getting Started: How to Succeed in Heritage Tourism." Designed to be used as a primer, the publication describes principles and steps that will help communities and regions interested in developing and managing heritage tourism. (Available from the National Trust for Historic Preservation, 511 Sixteenth Street Suite 700, Denver, Colorado 80202, USA.)

10

Heritage Tourism and Community
Development: Lessons from Historic Rugby

Benita J. Howell

Heritage tourism was a key theme in the flurry of planning for Tennessee's Bicentennial and the 1996 Olympic Games. Much groundwork for showcasing local culture and history was laid during the three years of preparation for the Tennessee Homecoming 86 celebration. Six anthropologists, historians, and folklorists supported by the Tennessee Humanities Council helped members of local Homecoming committees discover the unique features of their towns, write proposals for funding, engage in research, prepare and mount exhibits, and stage local festivals (Duggan 1990). When the Homecoming projects were complete, local organizations such as the Etowah Arts Council and the Community Action Group of Englewood (CAGE) directed their energies and newly acquired skills toward longer-term goals. In the case of Etowah, Homecoming 86 created a permanent exhibit on the town's connection with the L&N Railroad and restored the depot to house the exhibit. Etowah's depot museum became a center for various arts activities. Linda Caldwell, who headed the Etowah Arts Council, went on to direct the Tennessee Overhill Experience, a regional heritage tourism project that seeks to replicate Etowah's success in more than half a dozen other places in McMinn, Monroe and Polk counties to put them on the map collectively as a regional tourist destination (Caldwell 1994).

Tennessee Overhill Experience is but one of many recent heritage tourism developments in our state, and similar attractions are being cultivated all across the United States (see, for example, Feintuch 1988; Howell 1990; Hufford 1994). Business and political leaders in small towns hope that heritage tourism will make nostalgia for the past pay dividends in future economic development. The bandwagon is in motion, and everyone seems to be jumping on. Can all of them realize their aspirations and avoid undesirable consequences?

Anthropologists may assist heritage tourism planning by identifying, documenting, and interpreting the history and elements of traditional culture that have the potential to become visitor attractions. On the other hand, as everyday observers and students of cultural interaction and culture change, we cultural specialists have had ample opportunity to see and describe how tourism can adversely affect host communities.

Patricia Beaver, for example, witnessed impacts of tourism on the Boone-

Blowing Rock section of Western North Carolina, where the majority of jobs created for local people have been low-skill, low-wage service jobs, and often seasonal (Beaver 1982). As corporately owned resorts, vacation homes, and retirement communities sprang up in Western North Carolina, competition between developers drove up land prices and tax assessments for local property owners. Tax rates also increased to help county governments pay for road improvements, necessary expansion of the water and sanitation systems, additional solid waste collection, and increased fire and police protection. Land-poor residents reluctantly sold family land, sacrificing both their sentimental attachment to the land and the chance to farm part-time as a buffer against layoffs from industrial jobs or seasonal employment. As additional mountain land came on the market, the pace of building tourism facilities accelerated. Crowding, traffic, noise, and visual pollution undermined residents quality of life and detracted from the mountain scenery visitors came to enjoy.

Short-term tourists, and perhaps especially the outsiders who become residents in rural areas, may find local ways quaint, charming, puzzling, or irritating by turns. But knowingly or not, intentionally or not, their presence hastens the demise of local customs and begins transforming the "different" place they have discovered into a place more like the one they came from. George Hicks, an anthropologist who has worked in Western North Carolina, explained the resentment his neighbors felt when newcomers fenced and posted wooded land that by tradition was open to anyone in the community (Hicks 1976). Another familiar institution is the country store. Hicks observed that while visitors enjoy the old fashioned general store as a quaint museum/emporium, they want the self-service merchandising of convenience stores when they buy picnic and camping supplies. Local merchants change their ways of doing business, chain stores arrive, and soon the place looks like Any Crossroads, USA, with perhaps a Cracker Barrel Old Country Store now catering to nostalgia for the old-fashioned general store.

An extensive literature describes how traditional culture is transformed into a marketable commodity (i.e., country store into Cracker Barrel), but East Tennesseans do not need cultural specialists to tell them that the resulting stereotypes are often degrading. To understand "commoditization" of culture, just look at the hillbilly souvenirs sold in Pigeon Forge gift shops.

One of the most promising features of heritage tourism (in contrast to mass tourism) is its use of cultural resources as the *key attraction*, not just a veneer of "local color" to embellish mass tourism and recreation. The cultural resource to be conserved and interpreted to visitors is really the entire environment that gives a place its unique flavor, not just a few historic sites and the activities listed on a calendar of cultural events. Heritage tourism appeals to a smaller segment of the public than mass tourism destinations like Pigeon Forge or Dollywood. These tourists are generally older and more affluent than average and have more leisure time for travel. As the American population ages, this segment of the tourist market will expand. Nevertheless, communities should not fasten their hopes for economic revitalization on heritage tourism alone. Rather, tourism should be one element in a multifaceted strategy of building economic strength through diversification.

Tourism built on heritage resources seems especially able to enhance broad-based economic development because every amenity provided for visitors, whether museums, cultural events, or outlets for locally produced craft and food items, enhances local quality of life as well as the visitor's experience. In contrast to mass tourism, heritage tourism destinations must limit development and avoid crowding if they want to maintain an attractive ambiance. The payoff from small-scale tourism is a community more able to woo desirable corporate employers, support small business enterprises, provide employment to keep its brightest young people in the community, and attract well-educated and highly skilled new citizens. The National Trust for Historic Preservation's Heritage Tourism Initiative, Pennsylvania's plan for industrial heritage parks , and South Carolina's program to identify and interpret the cultural resources of its small towns are examples of this strategy (see Caldwell 1994; Davis 1991; Staub 1994). All of these programs envision heritage tourism not as an end point, but as the first step in diversified, sustainable economic development.

The vision of economic revitalization through tourism is alluring, but can all of the communities now jumping on the heritage tourism bandwagon achieve the level of excellence in historic interpretation that will impress visitors and generate strong word-of-mouth advertising? Will they shun overdevelopment and inappropriate development to preserve a total environment that will attract repeat visits? Will they address the broader community development issues they need to confront? These are important questions, perhaps better appreciated through positive examples than preaching on the perils and pitfalls of badly managed tourism development. One such positive example is Historic Rugby, an exemplary heritage tourism destination already familiar to many Tennesseans.

Rugby Past and Present

Located in the northernmost tip of Morgan County, Rugby was established in 1880 on land purchased by the Board of Aid to Land Ownership, Ltd, a group of financial backers who responded to British educator Thomas Hughes's plan to give younger sons of English gentry freedom to earn their living as farmers, craftsmen, and entrepreneurs. These young men were victims of the English social system, deprived of significant inheritance by the rule of primogeniture, and at the same time prevented by class consciousness from pursuing gainful employment in any except the gentlemen's professions—law, medicine, scholarship or the church. New Englanders wanting a fresh start in a planned community blessed with pleasant climate also became Rugbeians.

Rugby was carefully planned and the town laid out in advance of the colony's inauguration, but lack of practical farming and business experience and the constraints of poor soil and poor transportation undermined many of the economic endeavors that were supposed to sustain the colony. However, picturesque scenery and healthful summer climate made Rugby an ideal site for tourism from its earliest days. The Tabard Inn was probably the colony's most successful enterprise. Unfortunately, the inn burned in 1884, the same year Rugby's population peaked at approximately 300. Another fire destroyed the rebuilt Tabard Inn in 1900. The colony, already in decline by that time, was unable to finance another rebuilding of the inn.

A few of the original families maintained ties with Rugby and a few newcomers discovered it, but aside from an abortive effort to create a state park at Rugby in the 1930s, when the area was threatened by commercial timber cutting, the place languished until the 1960s. Brian Stagg rediscovered Rugby's past as a high school student in nearby Deer Lodge, about the time the federal Historic Preservation Act of 1966 legitimated such interests and authorized federal support for preservation activities.

Rugby soon took advantage of this improved national climate for heritage conservation. The Rugby Restoration Association, which formed in 1966, achieved National Historic District status for Rugby in 1972, making Rugby eligible for grants-in-aid to rehabilitate original buildings that were still standing. State legislation in 1972 established a Rugby Historic Commission. That step reflected governmental concern for protecting historic structures and controlling development to prevent negative impacts, but it left the authority and means for acting somewhat vague.

Authorization of the Big South Fork National River and Recreation Area (BSFNRRA) in 1974 made it imperative that Rugby's future not be left to chance. Without careful planning and regulation of development, Rugby would resemble the typical national park gateway more than the unique resource the Rugby Restoration Association hoped to protect. The simple solution would have incorporated the Rugby Historic District into the BSFNRRA, making it an architectural history resource similar to Cade's Cove in Great Smoky Mountain National Park, a "community" of buildings without people. But activists in Rugby Restoration Association argued that Rugby's significance lay not so much in the assemblage of Victorian buildings as in Hughes's "great experiment," his vision of a planned community where personal endeavors and the collective good would be mutually reinforcing and the dignity of all labor would be honored. The new Rugbeians wanted to foster that way of life as much as restore the physical colony. Interpreting Historic Rugby (the non-profit corporation's new name) ultimately meant recreating the living community Hughes had envisioned, a place where some of the original Rugbeians pursuits—primarily tourism, handicraft and arts enterprises—could thrive.

Rugby was left outside the recreation area boundaries on condition that the community, with technical assistance and financial support from the US Army Corps of Engineers, would assess the likely impact of increased tourism and formulate a management plan. The US Army Corps of Engineers funded the planning study in 1979. The Rugby Colony Master Plan was to specify historic preservation measures while at the same time encouraging compatible development so that Rugby could at long last realize its original ambitions as a planned, intentional community. A Nashville consulting firm, Building Conservation Technology, Inc., conducted a series of workshops with local residents and the general public in 1980–81. Their work culminated in 1986 with publication of *Master Plan for the Development, Management and Protection of the Rugby Colony Historic Area, Morgan and Scott Counties, Tennessee* (Building Conservation Technology 1986). In competition with more than 800 entries, the Master Plan won a First Award from *Progressive Architecture*.

Rugby's operations and staff have expanded greatly over the past twenty years. Beginning with guided walking tours of four original buildings, Rugby's attractions now include festivals and holiday celebrations, craft and book sales outlets, dining and lodging facilities, and elder hostel and workshop events that encourage overnight visits. Expansion has meant additional renovation and reconstruction of the buildings that house these activities. A restaurant, community building-library, and workshop have been built using designs and materials compatible with the original Victorian structures. Historic Rugby has been careful not to push the pace of reconstruction, but to proceed only when there is both good documentation and an immediate function for the building. Current priorities call for renovating the Hughes family home, Uffington House, as a tour site and reconstructing the Perrigo Boarding House for more overnight lodgings (Stagg interview 1994).

There are other historic homes and intrusive modern buildings within the Historic District (Stagg interview 1994). Historic Rugby acquires these properties as funds permit, not to retain title, but to attach restrictive covenants and resell to private owners who will rehabilitate or build within the Master Plan's guidelines. Sale proceeds finance additional property transactions. Beacon Hill, a part of Rugby's original town plan that was never built, was recently opened for construction of new homes. In keeping with the spirit of nineteenth-century Rugby, cottage industries will be permitted, even encouraged. The prospect of more year-round residents once again raises economic and other constraints of community building on the Plateau that defeated the original Rugbeians. There are still opportunities for several original stores on Central Avenue to be reconstructed as additional retail outlets for crafts, antiques, and the like, but history has taught Rugby that tourism is a fickle livelihood affected by many unforeseen events. Just as the Tabard Inn was gaining a following, a typhoid epidemic undermined its reputation as a healthful summer retreat. A healthy economy eluded old Rugby. Improved transportation, electronic technologies that facilitate decentralized work, and development in nearby towns offer hope that the revitalized community can build a sustainable economy.

Finding itself adjacent to the BSFNRRA has been a boon to Rugby. Federal agencies (originally the US Army Corps of Engineers and now the National

Park Service) became partners with Rugby in conserving the architectural resource and enhancing its tourism potential, and the national area ensured
greenbelt buffering on two sides. The original town plan and current Master
Plan emphasize green space, especially public recreational access to the scenic
corridor along Clear Fork and White Oak Creeks, and in this respect Rugby's
objectives coincide with BSFNRRA's mandate for natural resource conservation. The recreation area also offers new development opportunities to Allardt,
Jamestown, Huntsville, and Oneida, nearby towns that are important to Rugby's economic future.

Ingredients in Rugby's Success

The federal Big South Fork project was a stroke of good fortune, but Rugby
reaped the benefits only because of clear goals, effective management, and
patience.

Clear Goals and Priorities

With Beacon Hill, Rugby embarks on building the kind of community Hughes
intended. Economic development compatible with managing the Historic District is essential, but there is consensus that managed growth is preferable to a
tourism bonanza. Many residents of the area and leaders in Historic Rugby,
Inc., have personal ties to Old Rugby. Preserving their past and the colony's
ideals have always been their primary concern. The cultural resource was not
developed as a "hook" to draw in tourist dollars; rather tourism appeared to be
the most effective means to underwrite and publicize the historic preservation
effort. The membership of Historic Rugby, Board of Directors, Executive Director, and local residents developed consensus through the dialogue and problem solving reflected in the Master Plan. A goals and objectives statement updated in 1993 keeps priorities clear and progress on track. Detailed supple-
ments will augment the master planning process as needed. A landscape design
update is in process to control vehicular and pedestrian traffic, define green
space, and buffer private residential areas from public areas (Stagg interview
1994). With clear preservation goals, the supportive conservation presence of
the NRA, and an excellent Master Plan in place, Rugby is better able to resist
incompatible development or overdevelopment than towns with unclear or conflicted goals and expectations for heritage tourism.

Creative Management and Grantsmanship

History has taught Rugby that tourism is not a "sure thing" but is subject to
fluctuations in the national economy, travel trends, and unforeseen factors like
old Rugby's typhoid epidemic and Tabard Inn fires. Historic Rugby, Inc. expe-

rienced steadily increasing museum admissions while building and expanding programs during the 1980s, but those increases leveled off during the recent recession. Rugby cushioned itself somewhat against unpredictable museum and tour revenues by increasing special festival and holiday events, expanding sales of books and handicrafts, improving dining and adding lodging facilities, and sponsoring elder hostels and workshops that generate overnight visits (ibid.). Revenues from dining, lodging, and sales outlets have continued to rise, reflecting the success of these activities in attracting both newcomers and providing amenities for regular visitors, especially those from neighboring communities. Increased construction and services could not be supported solely by revenues they generate, however, not even in the best economic times. Furthermore, every expansion in properties entails budgeting for maintenance. By extending restrictive covenants to private properties, Historic Rugby both stretches its budget for restoration and reconstruction and supports the concept of attracting perhaps 300 residents who will have a stake in revitalizing community life. This approach works because the planning process involved local property owners and won their support. Historic Rugby, Inc. and its management structure withstood a leadership challenge in 1990 and seem to have emerged stronger than ever.

As a National Register historic district and a museum constantly upgrading its resources, interpretation, and research capacity, Rugby has won impressive grant funds to invest in continued improvements. After the Big South Fork project was authorized in 1974, the Department of the Interior and the Corps of Engineers became significant sources of grant funds and technical assistance, but Executive Director Barbara Stagg has pursued support energetically and made creative use of varied funding sources: CETA and the Emergency Jobs Bill for staff, TVA economic development funds to start up lodging facilities and a craft outlet, and most recently a Community Development Block Grant of over $450,000 for restoration and construction of buildings, sponsored by the neighboring incorporated town of Allardt. Additional grant funds have come from various state agencies and private foundations, from the Institute for Museum Services, and the National Endowment for the Humanities. Progress towards implementing accepted museum procedures and gaining museum accreditation has made Historic Rugby more competitive in seeking grants from these sources. Maintaining the integrity of the resource and enhancing it with top quality interpretation does pay. Rugby's impressive record of grants has been thus summarized: "In 23 years Rugby received $1.4 million in grants from 18 organizations. Five of these organizations gave more than one grant, eight gave gifts over $25,000, and three of the gifts were over $100,000. Individual gifts, bequests, and the Second Century Campaign (for donations matched by state and federal grants) have built an endowment to support maintenance and continued development of Historic Rugby's properties" (Horton 1990).

Patience

Rugby's program of architectural restoration and heritage tourism is almost three decades old, the result of persistence and hard work as well as good planning and management. Patience is one lesson to learn from Rugby's experience, and one expressed in the inaugural address Thomas Hughes gave at the colony's official opening on 5 October 1880:

> Whether the lands will double or quadruple in value before you have fairly learned how to live on them; whether you will make five, or twenty, or one hundred percent on your investments, we offer no opinion. You can judge for yourselves of the chances, if these are your main aims. Speaking for myself, however, I must say that I look with distrust rather than with hope on very rapid pecuniary returns. I am old fashioned enough to prefer slow and steady growth....
>
> So far as I have been able to judge, (other) new settlements are being, as a rule, dwarfed and demoralized by hurrying forward in the pursuit of gain, allowing this to become the absorbing propensity of each infant community. Then follows, as surely as night follows day, that feverish activity of mercantile speculation which is the great danger and, to my mind, the great disgrace of our time (Hughes 1881:105–6).

Far from being caught up in the a boom of mineral and timber development, the Cumberland Plateau continued to be sparsely populated and underdeveloped in comparison with the rest of the state. Nevertheless, when Highway 52 was improved and paved in the 1950s, it followed old Central Avenue through the center of Rugby. Highway 52 now carries noisy coal and log trucks and oilfield service equipment within a few yards of residences and the site of the Perrigo Boarding House now slated for reconstruction. As early as 1971, Brian Stagg began lobbying for a by-pass; finally, twenty-three years later, bidding is underway on the first phase of construction.

While it removes the most worrisome intrusion from the Historic District, the bypass itself will provide a locus for non-conforming structures and businesses like service stations and fast food restaurants that would be out of place in the Historic District. Just this summer, Historic Rugby was able to purchase land between the bypass corridor and the Historic District with donations from Stokely Foundation and Cracker Barrel Old Country Store and a low-interest loan from the National Trust for Historic Preservation. The 151-acre Allerton tract will permit extension of Rugby's trail system while functioning as a greenbelt separating the Historic District from commercial development along the bypass (Stagg interview 1994). From the vantage point of 1994, all of the pieces in the Master Plan's zoning scheme seem to be falling into place, but it took many years of effort and patience, working with state and federal agencies, private land owners, and benefactors to achieve this goal.

Linking the Past and the Future

Small-scale ecotourism, planning, and hopes for prudent, sustainable growth are integral parts of the original Rugby colony's legacy. There is consistency in activities as well as outward appearance between the Victorian colony and the contemporary community of the Second Century. Sustainable heritage tourism requires the kind of planning, management, and dedication to resource protection that Rugby displays. The challenge for Rugby's Second Century is community development, working in partnership with Big South Fork and neighboring towns to stimulate economic development compatible with cultural and natural conservation. The Beacon Hill development signals that Rugby is poised to face the community development challenge that defeated it a century ago. Rugby lives by learning from its past. Other communities contemplating cultural tourism can learn from Rugby too.

Appreciation

Many thanks to Barbara Stagg for graciously granting an interview in the midst of a busy summer season and for providing copies of recent documents that update the Master Plan. She also suggested that Thomas Hughes had words of caution for those obsessed with "rapid pecuniary returns." Brief summaries of Rugby's history can be found in Dickinson's general history of Morgan County (Dickinson 1987) and in Manning's guide to recreation and tourism attractions on the Cumberland Plateau (Manning 1993). For a more detailed analysis of economic and other factors contributing to the original colony's failure, see Miller (1941). Horton's (1990) leaflet is an excellent summary of Rugby Restoration Association/Historic Rugby's goals and accomplishments between 1966 and 1989. Historic Rugby's quarterly newsletter for members, *The Rugbeian*, is the best source for news of recent developments. Information about memberships, special events, and lodging can be obtained by writing or calling Historic Rugby, PO Box 8, Rugby, TN 37733, (615) 628-2441.

References

Beaver, Patricia D. (1982) "Appalachian Families, Landownership, and Public Policy." In R.L Hall and C.B. Stack, eds. *Holding on to the Land and the Lord: Kinship, Ritual, Land Tenure, and Social Policy in the Rural South* (edited by Hall, R.L. and Stack, C.B.), 146–154. Athens: University of Georgia Press.

Building Conservation Technology, Inc. (1986) *Master Plan for the Development, Management and Protection of the Rugby Colony Historic Area, Morgan and Scott Counties, Tennessee.* Nashville: Building Conservation Technology.

Caldwell, Linda (1994) "Creating a New Community," *Touchstone* 26:8–12.

Davis, Joan (1991) "The South Carolina Cultural Conservation Consortium Project."
    Paper presented at the First South Carolina Cultural Conservation Conference, Sep-
    tember 29–October 1, 1991, at McCormick, SC.

Dickinson, W. Calvin (1987) *Morgan County.* Tennessee County History Series. Mem-
    phis: Memphis State University Press.

Duggan, Betty J. (1990) "New Ways for Old: Assessing Contributions of the Tennessee
    Community Heritage Project." In *Cultural Heritage Conservation in the American
    South* (edited by Howell, B.J.), 54–65. Athens: University of Georgia Press.

Feintuch, Burt, ed. (1988) *The Conservation of Culture: Folklorists and the Public Sec-
    tor.* Lexington: University Press of Kentucky, 1988

Hicks, George (1976) *Appalachian Valley.* New York: Holt, Rinehart and Winston.

Horton, Ruth (1990) "Rugby, Tennessee" Thriving Hometown Networks File Number
    012. Washington, DC: National Association of Towns and Townships, 6.

Howell, Benita J., ed. (1990) *Cultural Heritage Conservation in the American South.*
    Athens: University of Georgia Press.

Hufford, Mary, ed. (1994) *Conserving Culture: A New Discourse on Heritage.* Urbana:
    University of Illinois Press.

Hughes, Thomas (1881) *Rugby, Tennessee. Being Some Account of the Settlement Founded
    on the Cumberland Plateau.* London: Macmillan.

Manning, Russ (1993) *The Historic Cumberland Plateau: An Explorer's Guide.* Knoxville:
    University of Tennessee Press.

Miller, Ernest I. (1941) *The English Settlement at Rugby, Tennessee.* Rural Research
    Series Monograph 128. Knoxville: University of Tennessee College of Agriculture.

Stagg Interview (1994) Benita Howell Interview with Barbara Stagg, Rugby, 18 August.

Staub, Sholom (1994) "Cultural Conservation and Economic Recovery Planning: The
    Pennsylvania Heritage Parks Program." In *Conserving Culture: A New Discourse on
    Heritage* (edited by Hufford, Mary), 229–244. Urbana: University of Illinois Press,
    1994.